More Memories of Stoke-on-Trent

Edited by Syd Bailey

The publishers would like to thank the following companies for their support in the production of this book

Main sponsor
Spode

E Cartlidge Limited

Churchill China plc

A H Davey (Roadways) Limited

The Diamond Tile Company Limited

Goodwins Jewellers

Hadida

Daniel Platt Limited

Portmeirion Potteries Limited

Trent Bathrooms

JH Weatherby & Sons Limited

First published in Great Britain by True North Books
Units 3-5 Heathfield Industrial Park,
Heathfield Street, Elland HX5 9AE
Telephone: 01422 377977

ISBN 1 903204 12 7

Text, design and origination by True North Books Limited
Printed and bound by The Amadeus Press Limited

Introduction

Modern Stoke-on-Trent has entered the 21st century as a thriving city. Created from the joining of the six Potteries' towns into a federation early last century, it became the centre of the ceramics trade, with some additional involvement in mining, the rubber industry and iron and steel. Coal and steel production, though, was drastically cut back in the late 20th century. Inside this book you will find a selection of carefully chosen images on every page. To back them up are captions and articles that help the reader recall what life was like in the 20th century. Photographs and descriptions of streets and buildings that have long gone give a flavour of how we used to live. For younger readers the book will make sense of the stories their parents and grandparents have told them. For the reader of more mature years, this is the ideal way to bring back those childhood memories. As you leaf through the pages, remember the way life was.

Those half forgotten pictures in the deepest recesses of your mind will jump to the front of your brain once more. Stimulated by the delightful pictures, the memory will be able to take charge and firm up what we thought we could recall. In some cases it might be that our thoughts were just flights of fancy. This book will decide once and for all. Was the Angel next to the Grapes, or was it the Swan? The camera never lies and this book will decide the issue. It might also provoke argument and discussion about events that surrounded the captured images. What they will definitely do is bring back a wave of joy and nostalgia as the reader turns each page and lives again the century that saw Stoke-on-Trent emerge in its own right.

Although we all know that Stoke-on-Trent came into being in the last century, it did not appear overnight. Historians and archaeologists can place habitation as far back as 10,000 years ago. The oldest settlement was on the hilltop at Penkhull. However, the pebbly sandstone and heavy clay soil meant that the nearby land was badly drained. This made it unsuitable for good cultivation. In a time when agriculture was the main way of life, this meant that settlements were few and far between. It is ironic that this sort of land would be the main reason for the growth of the Potteries in more recent times. Then it would be the richness of the underlying rocks to the industrialist that fed the rise in importance of the area. How things change. What our ancestors thought were unworkable conditions thousands of years ago became important to the economic wealth of latterday times. Coal deposits, ironstone for iron ore, clay for ceramics and sandstone for concrete changed the way Britain looked at the value of the ground beneath its feet.

Romans trod that ground 2,000 years ago. It seems that they were firing a pottery kiln at Trent Vale in 70 AD. Coins, bits of pottery, metal and glass connected to those times have been unearthed by digs around Staffordshire. Most of the material discovered was the property of the well to do. The poor had few possessions. Jewellery, fine pottery and neatly worked glassware belonged to the ruling classes. Evidence of their homes, built from brick and stone, remain. The wattle and daub of the peasants disappeared quickly. However, some evidence of their rough pottery and agricultural implements has been found to tell us how they lived. One of the most important of the excavated sites was at Rocester, a few miles southeast of what is now Alton Towers. Cynics might find that sort of connection between Roman civilisation and the modern theme park amusing, to say the least! Even in those times, people who lived in the area were still few and far between. Their existence as simple farmers carried on regardless of the invasion from Caesar's forces and those that followed. Some took notice, as they had no alternative. A number were whisked off into slavery. Life may have been hard tilling the poor soil, but, sent to other parts of the Roman empire, they must have longed for their homeland when literally slaving away for their new rich masters.

By the time of the 1086 Domesday Book, Penkhull had become established as a clearly defined village. It remained an important place right through into the 19th century. However, Stoke did not get a mention, although there was a church recorded in the vicinity.

Covered by the Forest of Lyme, the district was home to animals rather than man. Cistercian monks settled at Hulton Abbey in 1223 and mined a little coal and made a few pots. This was the beginning of a new age but it was a while coming; Tunstall Manor records only mention pottery manufacture in 1348. Tunstall can claim to be the oldest of the six towns that went to form modern Stoke-on-Trent, though Burslem has long disputed the title. By the 17th century both these villages were producing earthenware. Longton did not begin to take part in the industry until the following century. Hanley, Stoke and Fenton were still agricultural areas until the same time, when the Industrial Revolution changed it all. The population of the Potteries had been measured in hundreds, rising to about 4,000 overall in 1738. By the start of the 19th century, that figure had multiplied sixfold and the census of 1841 recorded a population of 68,000. This explosion in development was largely thanks to the great ceramics industry. Josiah Wedgwood, Josiah Spode and Herbert Minton led the way in mass producing fine pottery and porcelain that had developed from the cottage and backyard industries. New turnpike roads and the canals of James Brindley opened up export routes to the rest of the country and beyond. The six towns grew in importance as iron, steel and coal were produced. By the 19th century each had its own commissioners for local services and talks were held on how to combine their efforts as the 20th century began. The modern age of Stoke-on-Trent was about to dawn.

Now, pick up a glass, sit well back in that armchair, turn over the page and enter a paradise of nostalgia.

Contents

The Warrillow Collection

The streets of change

The railway bridge at Longton, seen in 1930, offered advice on the benefits of drinking Bass. To suggest that it should become a habit would be difficult to get past advertising censors in this day and age. If the slogan set the passerby's mind thinking about a pint, then the Crown and Anchor Hotel opposite was handily placed. Bass had a campaign at the time featuring a cartoon character called Bill Sticker. He was seen pasting the various slogans thought up by the brewery advertising team in a series of unusual places. One showed him at work on the pyramids in Egypt! Longton railway station had been part of the North Staffordshire Railway Company. The NSR was known as the 'Knotty' to locals. From its beginnings in 1846 the Knotty built local railways that linked the Potteries towns with the national network. This helped local industry find wider markets as the canal system had taken the bulk of the freight until then. The railway also brought the seaside closer. In later days excursion trains to exotic resorts like Llandudno would be filled with happy trippers. The company merged with the London, Midland and Scottish Railway in 1923. Gradually, the NSR influence lessened. Other companies, including the L&NWR at Crewe, absorbed different sections. After World War II, nationalisation meant that the separate identities railway companies enjoyed was to be lost forever.

The Warrillow Collection

The Warrillow Collection

Left: Looking towards Charles Street Chapel, near to Parliament Row, the smoky atmosphere that was Hanley in 1948 can be seen quite clearly, if that is the right word. The chapel and next door Chatterley House were demolished in 1960-61. That was a pity as the city lost one of its most attractive places of worship. The interior was a particular delight. Along the street shoppers were out in force. The fancy goods shop held all sorts of delights, though not everything could be described as fancy. Often it was a good excuse to label those items that defied classification in such a way. The shop was a good place to pick up something slightly out of the ordinary. It was just the sort of place to pop into for a one-off present for your granny. What she thought of it was not the point! The fancy goods shop came back into its own in these early postwar years. We stopped bothering with them when the balloon went up. Then it became more important to use only what was necessary. But how nice it was to be able to relax and indulge in buying something that was not quite a luxury but an item that was a little light hearted. The grimy fumes from the chimneys that billowed above the shoppers would not be allowed to continue unchecked. During the next decade or two Parliament and local government would see to that.

Above: This was Basford Bank as it looked in 1949. Garner Street is away to the left. Petrol rationing was still biting in those few short years after the war. Not a car in sight; just a solitary van making its peaceful way down the slope. Economy was the name of the game. For those of us who had cars, the meagre petrol ration had to be used sparingly. Only essential journeys were made. The motorbike used a lot less fuel and many turned to two wheels rather than four. Some were equipped with sidecars so that the family could be carried around. They were not particularly safe in those vulnerable contraptions, but there was less traffic on the road to worry about. It is a different story in the 21st century. But, needs must and, so, back then, we wheeled out the pushbike or set off on foot if motor transport was not for us. People were well used to travelling via 'Shanks's pony'. There had been plenty of time to practise in the 1940s. Many children grew up in homes that had never owned a car and they quite happily carried bags and set off up hills without a thought. Contrast that with the modern family. Two car homes are the norm. Kids are ferried everywhere. They cannot even get the few yards to school under their own steam any more. How more peaceful it was in 1949. Pedestrians even had time to hold conversations and cyclists could look at the countryside.

Bottom: Burslem had been one of the worst slum areas in the region during the middle of the 19th century. It took a while to change. Eventually, some 1,500 new houses were built around Moorland Road and in the town to improve both the town's appearance and the living conditions. A century after being described so poorly, by 1957 Burslem could boast more about its heritage as the 'mother town of the Potteries' than the squalid parts of its past. It had not been alone in having poor social conditions. However, under Harold Macmillan's Tories, this woman pausing outside the food speciality shop of B Adams Ltd had a good home to live in and money in her purse. The immediate postwar days of austerity and widespread rationing had gone. The corner had been turned and Britain was entering a new age of prosperity. The days of widespread car ownership were at hand, but not quite yet. This car-less view is one we will never see again as every spare piece of tarmac becomes clogged with bigger and shinier new models. As the woman glances in the shop window she must have thought what a treat it was to have a choice. For well over a decade she had been limited to a few ounces of meat, sugar and butter each week. Now, not only were these in plentiful supply, but she could add to them a feast of the more exotic. The greengrocer down the road even had bananas and pineapples!

Right: Walking up from the Trent and Mersey Canal in October 1960, these three lads had their backs to a depressing, but productive, skyline. At Shelton Bar, the Shelton Iron and Steel Works offered them employment. The alternative was to go into mining. Wedgwood's Etruria Works had gone and, for many, it was a choice on leaving school between one dirty job or another. The 4th Earl of Granville started to build three furnaces in 1839 and formed the Shelton Iron and Steel Company in 1888 which lasted for more than a century before it closed. Pig iron, steel joists, channels and angles were its main products. The factory was modernised in 1966, but gradually declined in importance as the 20th century drew to a close. When Josiah Wedgwood came to Etruria he said that he intended to build a model village that would be an example for other industrialists to copy. The housing came quickly. He had somewhere for his workers to live. Amenities like bakehouses and schools took longer to arrive. When Shelton Iron and Steel Works joined up on the site, it made the Wedgwood plans for further improvements impossible to achieve. Collieries added to the pollution and the area was a filthy place in which to live. People living over on the far side of the canal, at Basford Bank, complained bitterly of the noise. They worried about safety.

The Warrillow Collection

The Warrillow Collection

This is a Piccadilly view of Hanley rooftops taken in July 1951. The crowded buildings vie for space, their roofs and spires stretching to the heavens as though searching for air. The six towns of the Potteries grew quickly and haphazardly during the 19th century. The cramped nature of the various town centres was a reflection of the need to build and build quickly to accommodate the swiftly rising population. Hanley was little different from its fellow towns. Away from the town centre, the housing was just as crowded. Much of the housing was put up in order that it could be rented out. The more that could be crammed in, the greater the profit. Living conditions were poor. Sanitation was grim. Outdoor and open privvies stank and were an obvious source of disease. In Victorian times what sewers there were were often clogged. Water supplies were poor and often foul. Diarrhoea and typhoid were rife. As the workers earned low wages diets were inadequate. It was a vicious circle only broken when social reformers stepped in. The Duke of Sutherland was one of those who took charge. By the beginning of the 20th century clean two up two down housing and properly organised Health Boards had improved life no end. As can be seen in the distance in this photograph, not every health hazard was attended to. Smoke and air pollution had only recently become a major issue. Some of the buildings had layers of grime that had been gathering since the turn of the century and beyond. Holy Trinity Church is pictured in the centre, with the Odeon Cinema, the Sentinel office and the roof of the Empire Cinema to the right.

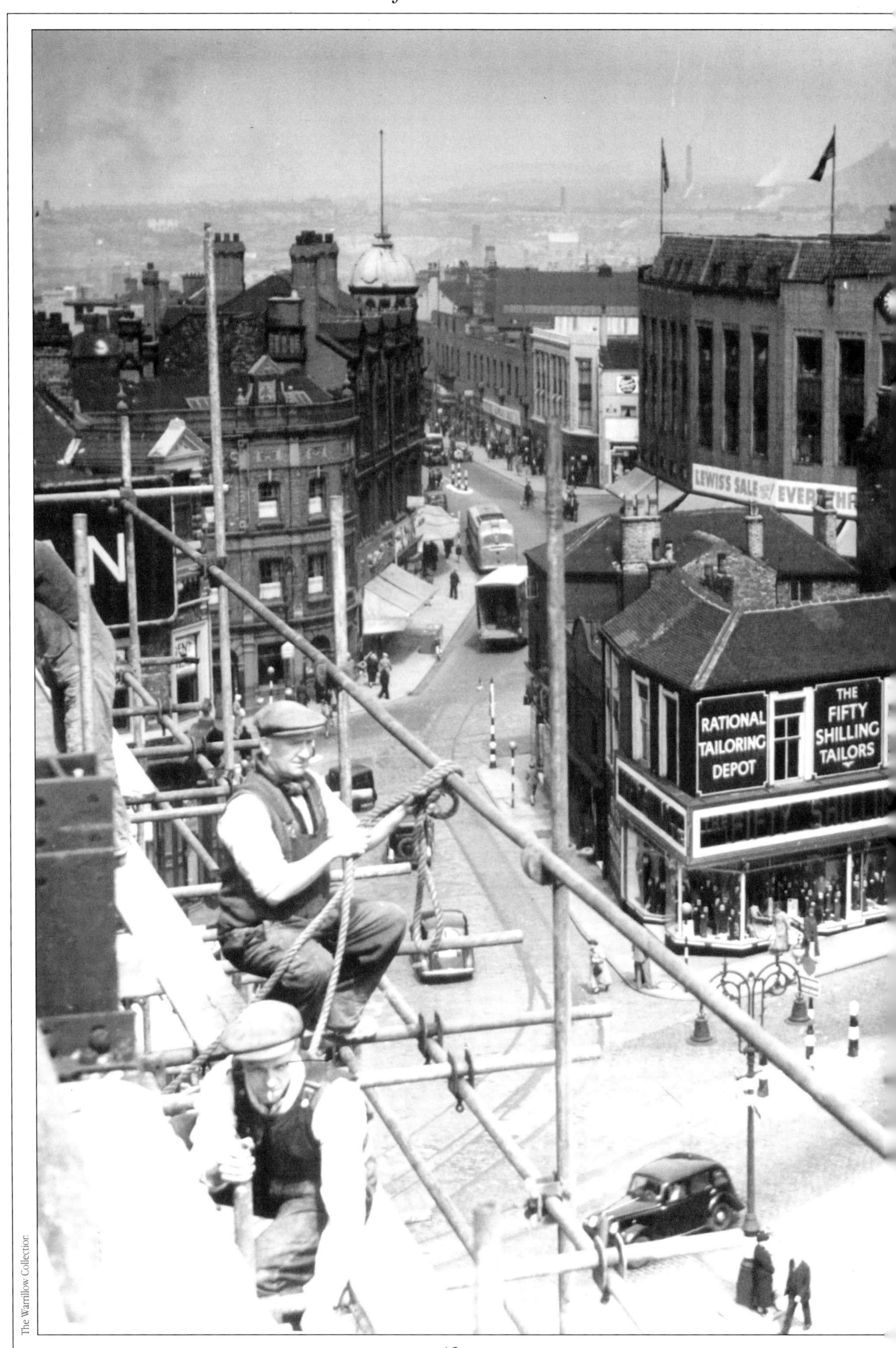

The Warrillow Collection.

High above Crown Bank these Hanley workmen were taking their lives in their hands. Health and safety Officials would have a field day with these chaps. They must be breaking nearly every regulation in the modern book. Flat caps instead of hard hats, a fag end jutting from the corner of a mouth and open scaffolding would cause an immediate stop notice to be placed on the job. But this was 1945. They had lived through six years of muck and bullets. If Hitler had not got them, then the council and its rules would be no problem. The tower of Hanley church can be seen jutting above the rest of the skyline. In the centre of the photograph the 50 bob tailor and Burton's men's outfitters would soon be doing good business. When the war ended ex-service personnel went there for their demob suits. Getting a complete range of clothing from Montague Burton was known as getting 'the full Monty'. The term came to mean something else after the film of that name came out over 50 years later. Much of the area has now been pedestrianised. Many of the shops gave way to the Potteries Shopping Centre. The Fifty Shilling Tailor name could not survive inflation. It is doubtful that, after 1971, it could have put up with being the Two Pounds Fifty Pence Tailor. It just doesn't sound right.

The Warrillow Collection

Above: Broad Street in Hanley is now part of the Cultural Quarter. In 1950, when this scene was captured, the long shadows had settled on a decade that had brought so much heartache. At this midpoint of the century it was time to look forward. The 50s would be a decade that saw prosperity return to the country. Lifestyles changed with the development of labour saving devices in the home. Electrical appliances like fridges, irons, vacuum cleaners, washing machines and cookers became commonplace. Televisions began to appear in the majority of homes and made the world shrink to the size of a 14 inch screen. Satellites flew in space and killer diseases were held in check. There were still warnings of the troubled past. The cold war and nuclear weapons saw to that, but it was a brighter time than the one we had left behind. During the previous half century Hanley had risen in importance. After 1910, when the federation of the six towns came into effect, Hanley developed as the natural centre of the new town. When Stoke-on-Trent achieved city status in 1925 it could rightly call itself the city centre. In its past days Hanley was an important mining town. There were slag heaps all around, but these have been landscaped or removed. As the 20th century unfolded it became the district's most important shopping centre. The redevelopment of the area that now houses the 1988 Potteries Shopping Centre has cemented that importance.

Above right: The District Bank on St John's Square, Burslem stood out on this sunny day in 1956. Perhaps the picture was taken on a Sunday, for there is little activity about. When we sit at our computers today and indulge in online banking, telephoned transactions and dot com financing, isn't it nice to look back at that institution that may one day disappear - the High Street bank? It will happen. It will also be in the name of progress. But, how reassuring the old bank was. Even the building looked secure. The way the District Bank dominated the picture inspired confidence. The building was solid. Therefore, so were its finances. You just had to have faith in the people who built and owned such a grand piece of architecture. The bank manager knew his customers. Potteries' folk knew the value of a shilling and the banker shared their ideas on thrift. Money was not to be splashed about, but be carefully managed. The man in the pin stripe suit had been brought up through the depressed inter war years. He was not about to let us squander our earnings on some frippery like an ostrich farm. The bank and its senior employee demanded and earned our respect. Sometimes, there was a little fear attached, especially if the chap in the rimless spectacles sent us a letter requesting a visit to discuss the little matter of our overdraft.

Below: Church Street, as seen from along London Road, is so named as it leads to Stoke's parish church, St Peter's. The bus is turning into Campbell Place, just opposite the Wheatsheaf Hotel. It is a busy street scene from 1955, when hemlines of coats and dresses were at about the same length. After the war, longer skirts became more popular. Women had to exercise caution in using cloth during the war years. Peacetime meant that more material could be used in clothing. Hemlines bounced up and down for the rest of the century. In the 60s they raced up the thigh when Mary Quant promoted the mini. Before long they were sweeping back down when the maxi skirt gained popularity. One constant was the witty Guinness advert. The crocodile and his 'my goodness, my Guinness' slogan was a long running favourite. Perhaps the best known was the toucan and 'You know what toucan do'. The bird with the colourful saw-edged bill still makes appearances on hoardings today. Slogans like 'Guinness is good for you' and a series of clever television adverts have made the drink into a household name. Ever since 1799, the production of porter, the dark ale with a creamy head, has been the national beer of Ireland. In 1955 it launched the 'Guinness Book of Records', containing both praiseworthy and idiotic special feats. 'Getting the Bass habit' was the rival slogan of one of its main competitors.

Bottom: Fronting onto Market Square, Hanley drinkers had a good choice in 1958. There was the Angel Hotel where thirsts could be slaked. If Bass was your tipple, then the Grapes was only next door. Pubs in the 1950s had names that meant something. They were named after famous people, events, places or activities. What on earth is the attraction or the connection with anything in a bar called the Flippin' Frog, the Wacky Winkle or some such other crazy modern idea? The interiors are all designed for lads who have yet to shave and girls fresh out of the pram. Conversation is a thing of the past. Even if any of these callow youths have anything worth saying they cannot be heard above the din that calls itself rap, funk or garage music. Garbage music, more like. Back in the 50s, when beer was beer and Wet, Wet, Wet was a term of derision, the local was a place to argue the relative merits of Stoke City and Port Vale, play darts, discuss the government's progress and get away from the missus.

There is plenty to remind us of how Stafford Street, Hanley looked in the 1950s. Many memories of the Palace Cinema, on the right, come flooding back. Cuddling on the back row with a sweetheart, some of us actually saw parts of James Dean's film 'Rebel Without a Cause'. Issued just a few months after his death, it became a cult movie and box office smash. The Palace had once been a skating rink. The atmosphere was much warmer when Dean's sultry good looks were projected onto the big screen. Above and beyond the cinema you can see the Albion Hotel, St John's CE School and the shops that gave way to become the bus station. The Post Office stands at the top left of the picture. The tower of the old Hanley High School is poking out above it all. The row of cottages that the buses are passing has long gone. The little line of public transport seems to prove the old saying: a bus does not come for ages, then, three come along all together. If you had the choice of these, surely you would pick the double decker to ride in. There is a new world to found from the top deck. At street level, as you ride through a town, all that can be seen is a shop or office front. Get upstairs and a different picture unfurls. Now you can see the top storeys of Victorian architecture with their beautifully carved stonework and motifs. Forget the modern glass fronts below and concentrate on the feast of culture above.

The Palace Cinema on Stafford Street had once been a skating rink

Six into one really does go!

It was the author (Enoch) Arnold Bennett who misled most of Britain into thinking that Stoke-on-Trent was an amalgamation of five towns, not six. In his highly detailed novels of about a century ago he used the 'Five Towns' as a background for his stories. 'Anna of the Five Towns' was the first major novel, followed by 'The Old Wives' tale and 'Clayhanger'. As a man born in Hanley in 1867 he should have known better, but he did move to London as a young man and later lived in Paris. Perhaps the big city life played tricks with his memory.

The Warrillow Collection

A defence for Bennett can be mounted. 'Clayhanger' was not published until 1910. That was the year that Stoke-on-Trent was officially created. Quite how he came to forget the part that Fenton played in the formation of the federation, we will never know. Although short of obvious landmarks, the town had a distinct identity, lying between Stoke and Longton. One of its famous sons was Thomas Whieldon, one of the leading potters of the 18th century. Other influential men in that industry included Miles and Charles Mason, as well as the firm of F and R Pratt. They were based in Fenton.

The five towns that Bennett remembered were Hanley, Burslem, Longton, Tunstall and Stoke. Back at the start of the 1700s, before the rapid growth of the large scale pottery industry, they were all no more than little villages linked by a track. Known as The Lane, it meandered from Tunstall through to Longton, which was also known as Lane End. It was the borough of Newcastle under Lyme that had the greatest influence, in those days. The villages had little to do with each other and Tunstall to Longton must have seemed like a journey of epic proportions three hundred years ago.

The influence of the Industrial Revolution and improvements in road travel meant that the villages grew to the size of small towns by the start of the 19th century. By then, Hanley had grown in such size and importance as to be able to challenge Burslem's right to be regarded as the major centre of influence amongst the six towns. Hanley had the added advantage of being the rough geographical centre of the location.

As early as 1817 at a public meeting the separate communities came together to discuss co-operation on a number of administrative matters, including policing. Four years earlier, the townships of Hanley and Shelton had become a market town with responsibility for regulating and improving Hanley marketplace. This combination was made fully official in 1857 as the borough of Hanley. When the 1832 Reform Act created the parliamentary borough of Stoke upon Trent, with two MPs representing all the Potteries, the seeds of amalgamation were sown. It was Burslem that rejected the idea of a formal coming together in 1839. When Longton, in 1865, Stoke upon Trent, in 1874 and Burslem, in 1878, became boroughs in their own right, further moves to combine were afoot. In 1888 an attempt was made to form a new county, the County of the Potteries. Fenton and Tunstall UDCs were formed in 1894 and through the first years of the 20th century there were a number of investigations into the practicality of making a federation of the six towns.

With the passing of the Federation Act in 1910, Stoke-on-Trent came into being and the first council meeting took place under the guidance of its first mayor, Cecil Wedgwood. His name made a happy link with the past as the town looked to the future.

Below: This early wartime view of the Sneyd Arms was taken at a busy time. There were plenty of local Tunstall residents on the streets that day. As there was little traffic about, it is obvious that petrol rationing had kept the roads largely free from motor cars. The little lad swinging around the Belisha beacon would normally have been given a quick clip round the ear for messing about near the roadside. But, there was little chance of a Ford 8 or suchlike bowling him over. If there had been, mum would have given him a sharp reminder. Nowadays it is called child abuse. Sixty years ago we called it teaching him a lesson. Countless little boys grew up with permanently red ears proclaiming, 'It never did me any harm.' Elsewhere you can see evidence of the war in the lamppost markings. They had white bands painted on them to help people find their way around during the blackout. Often these markings appeared on telegraph poles and roadside kerbs as well. Tunstall is the most northerly of the six towns. It has a population of over 27,000. It is situated on a ridge looking further north towards the Cheshire border. It is the home town for the family clan of Adams potters. Evidence of some of the older ceramics and brick industries, going back to the middle ages, can be found on the outskirts of the town.

Right: Every town has a Wheatsheaf. It is one of the most popular pub names about. With its links to the days when Stoke was a largely rural area, the Wheatsheaf Hotel had been a regular meeting place for people coming to market or just popping into the shops. However, the hotel's roots did not go back to agricultural times. It was just the name that made you think it did. It owed its existence to the days of the turnpike roads. No doubt local farmers came to sup there, but it was opened in 1793 as a coaching inn. Travellers on the Nottingham-Derby-Newcastle road stopped at the Wheatsheaf for refreshment or overnight accommodation. Tired horses would be given a well earned rest. A new team was placed in harness and off the stage-coach would roll once more. The Wheatsheaf was also a stage for the light-post London coach. In 1963 it was time for change, as it was with many Stoke-on-Trent buildings in this era. In came the workmen and down came the Wheatsheaf. It was rebuilt as an inn with offices above. The area became known as Campbell's Place, in honour of old Campbell Works' potbank that was sited around here. The Majestic Cinema, built in 1914, occupied a place where pottery had once been thrown. In 1924-27 Radio Stoke-on-Trent broadcast from the cinema. It was the area's first local radio station. The Majestic closed in 1957.

The Warrillow Collection

The Warrillow Collection

Above: For 800 years, from the days before the Domesday Book right up to Victorian times, nearly all of North Staffordshire was contained in the parishes of Stoke and Wolstanton. The present Wolstanton Church, designed to an early-English style, was built in 1623, and major alterations took place in 1860. In this photograph we are looking at the Stoke Parish Church of St Peter's. It is now marooned in a triangle formed by Glebe Street, Church Street and Queensway, the A500 motorway link road. In 1960 it was a more peaceful place, in keeping with its heritage. City Road led away to the right, towards Fenton and Longton. The leafy trees shrouded a long history. In the churchyard there is a small piece of an old cross. It has been dated as coming from Saxon times, perhaps before 1000 AD. Its existence has seen one millennium dawn and then close. The cross was used as a door lintel in the church that stood here in far off medieval days. Stonemasons and architects of our forefathers' days knew a thing or two about building things to last. It was not until 1830 that the church was knocked down and the present one erected. In Tudor times chapels were put up in Newcastle and Burslem. Monks had communities in Trentham, Newcastle and Hulton Abbey. Although John Wesley fired the population with religious zeal, the established church did not grow in strength until the 19th century. Churches were built in Hanley in 1738 and in Longton in 1761. Both were rebuilt before the end of the century, but Anglicans took another 50 years before their numbers swelled to any notable figure.

Below: The swinging '60s were about to begin as barmaids at the Swan Hotel pulled their final pints. One of Tunstall's older pubs was pulled down not long after this photograph was taken. Even 40 years ago, patterns were changing. The young had greater spending power than ever before. Hotels with mock Tudor frontages were not for the likes of those reared in coffee bars. They were now looking for evenings in the new dance clubs that would spring up in our cities. Beat groups and Carnaby Street clothing were just around the corner. Pubs even began to serve lager to men. Now that was a sign of the times. Another indicator of change lay across the road from the Swan. The self-service store had come to town. It marked the slow decline of the corner shop and speciality houses that dealt with just one line of goods. 'Pile 'em high and sell 'em cheap' was the new motto. 'The customer is always right' or 'We serve to please' went out of the window. Instead of walking a city's High Street, popping in a variety of shops, the housewife could do her weekly shop under one roof. Personal service gave way to saving time. Eventually, the supermarkets began to sell more than just food. Clothes shops felt the pinch. With the coming of the out of town hypermarkets and large shopping centres, people did not even have to go into town any more. Stoke-on-Trent has helped hold back that trend with Hanley's Potteries Shopping Centre. But, do not be surprised how your grandson answers a question about which sort of shop sells bananas. He is bound to say 'Tesco's.'

The Warrillow Collection

St Paul's Church was built in 1828. When it was knocked down in 1974, old pottery remains were found under its foundation stones. This view of it at Dale Hall, Burslem, was taken from an elevated position on the Catholic Church. Perhaps this was a sign of Christian togetherness that was to come. Around 1950, when this photograph was taken, there were still wide divisions between the different branches of Christianity that people followed. It was not uncommon for an Anglican family to want to have nothing to do with a 'left footer'. At the same time, Father Murphy was warning his flock about the dangers that mixed marriages brought to the immortal soul. John Wesley, that pioneer of the Methodist movement, visited Burslem in 1760. He attracted big crowds and an equally large following. After making several more visits, he sat for a portrait bust to be sculpted by Enoch Wood in 1784. Wesley had a permanent reminder of Burslem. His first visit had provoked an unruly element in the crowd to throw earth and stones at him. A facial scar was a permanent reminder that religion raises passions that are not always for the good. Methodism grew in the late 18th century at pace with the development of the Potteries. During the Victorian era, a return to Anglican principles developed. New churches were built and schools and nursing institutions owed their birth to such clergymen as Sir Lovelace Tomlinson Stamer. In the middle of the 20th century this work was continued by the Vicar of Etruria, Thomas Horwood, who helped set up Keele University. Catholicism was slow to develop until the influx of Irish immigrants in the mid 1800s.

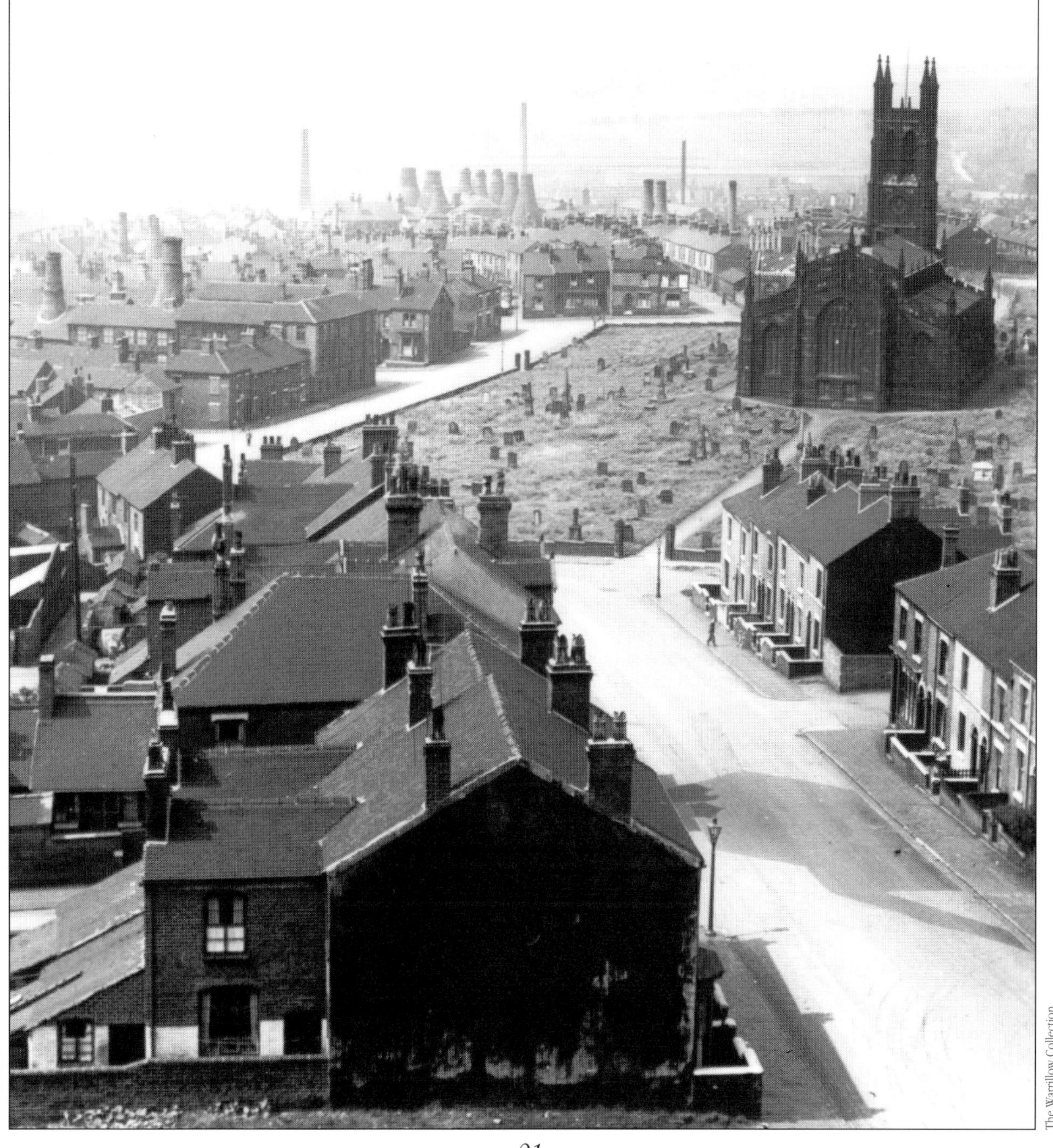

The Warrillow Collection

The Warrillow Collection

The Warrillow Collection

Left: At the time of writing thriving Hanley has a population of around 34,000. Longton has double that, but it is to Hanley that people turn as the city's heartland. Although Stoke-on-Trent has a total population of over a quarter of a million, when outlying districts are included, it is Hanley that is regarded as the city pulse. It lost some of its influence in 1974 when local government reorganisation took place. As well as creating new daft names for counties and wiping others off the map, this legislation handed over some of the city's services to Staffordshire. Happily, in 1997, when unitary authority status was achieved, these services were reclaimed from the county. Stoke-on-Trent could then get on with co-ordinating local services for the local people that it knew. In this photograph Hanley is seen from the offices of the Sentinel, the city's newspaper that took that name in 1873. It's proprietor was the aptly named Thomas Potter. The camera is pointing down to Fountain Square as it was in 1960. Always a busy area, it is now thronged with pedestrians protected from traffic. It has become a lively place for diners and shoppers, with a good variety of stores and restaurants close by. Even though the Potteries Shopping Centre finished off many market traders, some continued to operate in a traditional way. Whilst others moved into the new market arcade, some were able to continue setting up their stalls on Market Street and Fountain Square. The fountain no longer flows, but became a landmark and valued link with the old days.

Above: Trinity Street takes you out of Hanley, past the Hilton and on to Etruria Road towards Newcastle. If you were born in Stoke-on-Trent, then this is the thoroughfare that brings you into the city from that town down the road. On your journey you will pass Festival Park with its Waterworld, Superbowl, ski centre and multi-screen cinema. In the late 1950s there was no such centralisation of entertainment. Cinemas, theatres and dance halls were scattered around the city centre. Some of them remain, but they are the exception rather than the rule. The Odeon, to the right, built on the site of the old Grand Theatre, lasted until 1975 when it became a wine bar. Buildings were demolished or changed their use. Perhaps the biggest change to the city centre came in the late 1980 when the shopping area was altered so dramatically. In the days when cinema going did not mean going to Festival Park, you could have gone to the Empire, at the top of Piccadilly. It opened in 1910 and closed in 1956. Alternatively, there was the New Roxy, the former Imperial Picture Palace. It closed in 1961. Older readers might also remember the Gordon that closed around the same time. Two years later the Capitol went, after 38 years in business. Other names like the Grand and the Theatre Royal gave a special air of importance to their existence. Television was the main killer. Trinity Street has continued to attract visitors to enter Hanley for its varied attractions, but the face has changed, as has the style of entertainment.

Above: The small knot of men near the lamppost might have been discussing where to go for a pint. The Marquis of Granby pub, next to George Mason's store, had just closed down. This was Crown Bank in 1959 and if Macmillan had told us all that we had never had it so good, why had the pub closed? Quite a few hotels across the Midlands share the same name. Granby, a village halfway between Nottingham and Grantham, was immortalised when John Manners took his courtesy title. He was the eldest son of the Duke of Rutland. A British Army officer, he fought with distinction in Scotland during the 1745 rebellion. He gained further fame as a hero of the Seven Years' War (1756-63). As the commander of the armed forces he led the cavalry to a spectacular victories over the French in Westphalia and at Vellinghausen. He had become a Member of Parliament in 1754, a position he held until his death in 1779. Sadly, the hero died a debtor. The frustrated drinkers needed someone like the Marquis to ride to their aid and reopen the pub, but it was not to be. Where they were standing was an old set of toilets, just below the iron railings in the centre of Crown Bank. The cyclist has come down Stafford Street and is travelling towards the area that is now the Potteries Shopping Centre. The Midland Bank is the building to the left of George Mason.

Right: Bell and Nicolson occupied part of the site where the City Museum and Art Gallery now stands. Bell Pottery was behind here, on the corner of Hanley's Broad Street and Bethesda Street. The buildings were demolished in the mid 1950s, a few short years after this photograph was taken. The corner that the pram pushers have just left is now a confusing mixture of one way systems and bus only lanes. So many of the old buildings in this part of town fell victim to the bulldozer. Many had served out their time. In other parts of the city, housing programmes had to be launched to rid Stoke-on-Trent of its dirty and depressed image. It took the best part of 60 years to develop the estates that replaced the old slums. After the 1919 Housing Act work was begun at Basford, Abbey Hulton, Trent Vale and Meir. An official 15 year building programme got under way in 1924. Many families had been living two persons to a room. In 1930 another Act made plans for widespread slum clearance. Stoke-on-Trent was the first in the country to submit a housing improvement programme to the Ministry of Health. At long last, work got under way in 1936. By the time war broke out, 1,000 new homes per year were being built. The work was suspended during the war. It was not until the 1950s before it started again. Not before time. There were still 12,000 homes classified as being unfit for human habitation.

The Warrillow Collection

Right: As the A50 links Hanley and Burslem, it is difficult for the visitor to work out whereabouts Cobridge can be found. Its edges have become blurred over the years as Waterloo Road offers few clues as to boundaries. This family knew where it lived in 1955. Its roots were Cobridge through and through.
The children were part of the well known baby boom of the late 1940s. Families were reunited after the second world war. Menfolk had been away from home serving king and country on many a foreign shore. Wives and sweethearts waited faithfully, or so they said. On demob what better way to celebrate the return to normality? Babyfair and similar shops had a field day. Silver Cross prams were in great demand and happy grans-to-be picked up knitting needles and clicked away gladly. The birth rate soared. It is no surprise that in the 21st century the government is getting itself in a knot trying to cope with the pension arrangements of huge numbers who, in a few years, will be of retirement age. Such thoughts did not worry the family strolling along Waterloo Road. The lads were happy. One had a bike to pedal and his brother a pram to shove along. Whether it held a baby or the coal is not easy to see. The youngster doing the pushing would have preferred future warmth to a howling babe. Behind them, the other two were content to share the bond that mums and daughters have the world over.

Below: VE and VJ days had been celebrated. In 1946 the world tried its best to get back to normal. Etruria was no different. As the cyclist pedalled her way along the bottom of Station Bank she had the road to herself. Petrol was heavily rationed and the bike was a more practical way of getting about. As she rode past the bill hoardings she might have spared a thought for the products being advertised. What was the use of HP sauce if there was only a meagre ration of meat to pour it on? Even though Britain was no longer threatened by invasion or by having its young men blown apart on a foreign field, the world beyond the white cliffs of Dover was still unsettled. Change was everywhere. Peron was the new leader in Argentina. The King of Italy had abdicated. Riots broke out in India and Palestine. Ho Chi Minh became North Vietnam's president. Churchill referred to the Soviet Union as drawing an iron curtain across Europe. Over the second half of the 20th century many of these names would dominate the front pages. As our cyclist passed the rows of houses her thoughts would not have stretched so far afield. She worried about what to prepare for tea. The peacetime loaf was darker than the wartime bread. It was even rationed on the basis that manual workers needed more than white collar staff. There was a thriving trade in black market produce and forged coupons. Was this the world for which her husband and brothers had fought?

Above: The sign in the centre of the entrance to Pall Mall must have been placed there for idiots. Who in his right mind would have driven over the pile of debris in the middle of the street? To the right, the old City Museum was being demolished. The work took place in 1956. The museum had been extended in 1927 to include an art gallery. The old building was inadequate to house the collections of artefacts and treasures it had gathered. Ever since the war there had been a series of campaigns to update the museum or move it to a more appropriate spot. At last, the city agreed. A new building was erected where the Bell Pottery once stood, on Bethesda Street. It cost £46,000, but was still not really big enough. By the 1980s further development had taken place until it became the building we can see today. Looking along Pall Mall from Piccadilly, the old Town Hall can be made out in the distance. It was once the Queen's Hotel and was requisitioned as the Town Hall in 1888. When the new County Borough of Stoke-on-Trent came into being in 1910 Hanley became the commercial centre and the administration was handled from Stoke. The building on the left is now part of the Regent. It now hosts large shows and is Hanley's pride and joy as a centre for the performing arts.

Top: Tony Blair became the British prime minister in 1997. His fourth child was born in May 2000. What has Leo Blair got to do with a photograph taken over 30 years before his birth? The women walking along the damp pavement had never heard of Blair. They knew Lionel Blair, the popular dancer and entertainer of the day. This other chap meant nothing. Note the handbags clutched firmly in their grasp. Women never went anywhere without one. It was as much a statement of femininity as of practicality. The bus turning towards Longton, into Trentham Road from Belgrave Road, had to wait for the green light in later years. A set of traffic signals was installed in 1972. A lot of rerouting of traffic took place in the 1990s. Traffic bound for Leek and Derby or heading for the M6 was taken by ring road and bypass to relieve this spot and many others from congestion. The pub on the corner served beer from the local Joule's brewery. Like many others, it was bought out by one of the giants. The Lord John Russell was named after the man who served two spells as prime minister (1846-52 and 1865-66). Russell championed the cause of religious freedom for both English dissenters and Irish Roman Catholics. Have you got the connection with the photograph yet? Russell was the last prime minister to become a father whilst in office. The last, that is, until Tony Blair took his record.

Cooling waters in the summer of 1940 as the world burned in turmoil. Even in those torrid times children could still find the time and a place to enjoy themselves. Socks and shoes were abandoned and they splashed happily in the stream. Mum would have warned them about broken bottles and rusty bits of metal. It was a little risky to go paddling, in case you got a cut foot. But, life is not much fun if you do not take a chance or two. The two girls in the centre look like sisters. Their hair was kept in place with kirby grips and little plastic slides in tortoise shell colours. The boys wore jackets and ties, even on a day out. Short trousers were worn well into secondary school age. Their hair was cut short. It was examined regularly by Nitty Nora, the school nurse. Anything crawling up there and it was off home to get a bottle of foul smelling lotion. It drove out the creepy crawlies as much by smell as by ingredients. We do not know whether these children were natives. They might have been evacuees. When the war began, train-loads of children left the big cities. With luggage labels round their necks, they said a tearful goodbye to their parents and went to areas that would be safe from bombing raids. Stoke-on-Trent received evacuees from Manchester, Liverpool, Birmingham and London. They were billeted with families paid a few shillings a week to offer them shelter. There were many tearful nights and a few wet beds as youngsters pined for home.

The Wardlow Collection

Out and about

Above: Looking a little windswept these girls are taking a carefree stroll along the towpath of the Trent and Mersey Canal. A stiff wind is whipping up the waters. Soon it will blow the storm clouds of war across the horizon. It is 1939 and Mr Chamberlain's famous little bit of paper, brought back from Munich, has turned out to be useless. The promise of peace in our lifetime was a hollow one. Children had walked this path for years. With their smart socks and frocks they dressed like little girls ought. They did not need to ape the pouting models and pop stars that make this century's kids old before their time. A bracing walk away from the smoking factory was the sort of entertainment that the modern Miss would sniff at. How much simpler it was in the childhood days of people who will now be senior citizens. Little things gave so much pleasure. They could count the number of locks that they passed on their walk and keep a record of the number of houseboats and barges they saw. Jolly bargees would wave and smile as they made their way from Runcorn, through Burslem and on to the River Trent. The brightly decorated barges with their hand painted pots and jugs were a feature of the canal. Children loved to see them negotiating the locks. The water rushing in and out, through the paddle gates, was a wonder of engineering that fascinated them. There was plenty of opportunity to see them. The canal rose and fell through a series of 75 such steps.

Above: Three generations enjoying a family time in Hanley Park. Dad is educating the little girl. His haircut and glasses are reminiscent of the 1950s. Short back and sides at the barber's, with a dab of Brylcreem, was all it took. Perms, blow waves, highlights and streaks for men were but a far off twinkle in the hairdresser's eye. Dad is explaining the Stoke-on-Trent coat of arms to his daughter. She is too young to be interested, but she is going to hear all about it, just the same. The Stafford Knot, either side of the boar's head, was taken from the Tunstall coat of arms. The knot was a design found on the shaft of the stone cross found in the parish churchyard, dating back over 1,000 years and is particularly associated with the 14th and 15th century Stafford family. The boar was part of the Copeland family coat of arms and appeared on that of Stoke upon Trent. Burslem was represented by the vase, Fenton by the fretty cross in the middle and Longton by the eagle, from the crest of James Glover. The dromedary came from Hanley, or its connection did! Tunstall and Burslem both provided the scythe. The symbols all showed some aspect important to the Potteries. The Portland vase was one of Wedgwood's most famous copies. The scythe linked with the agricultural past. The camel, as a beast of burden, provided support and the eagle went back to Roman times when it appeared on the legions' standards.

Above right: In November 1957 the children would have enjoyed setting off their ripraps, Roman candles and Vesuvius fountains. Catherine wheels had been pinned to a post so that they could spin freely. They never did. Dad had hammered the nail in too tight. The thing just fizzed and stayed still. Other years he did not hit it hard enough and the firework fell on the ground, turning wildly and showering everyone with sparks. Little tots held sparklers and weaved patterns into the cold night air. Mum shouted to keep them away from our eyes. For days before the children had propped up an old bundle of rags against the wall and asked people passing by for a penny for the guy. The bonfires sent smoke into a sky that was only just clearing, thanks to the Clean Air acts. It was a time for treacly parkin, oatcakes and sticky toffee. Potatoes were blackened in the embers of the fire and we all had a grand time. The fire services were on alert, because there was always someone's shed bursting into flame as stray rockets fell to earth. Perhaps these children had paused in St John's Square, near Fountain Place, on their way home from a friend's Guy Fawkes' celebration. They were looking at the old drinking fountain. It was a lovely piece of craftwork. The lamp on top was supported to two intertwining dolphins. Not surprisingly, we called it Dolphin Fountain.

RJ Mitchell's Spitfires were soon to be taking to the skies to defend the right of these lads to fish the Trent and Mersey Canal in peace. In the summer of 1940 we all became only too well aware of the war. Our troops had returned from Dunkirk, the Channel Islands had been invaded and the Luftwaffe began attacking shipping in the Channel. Whilst this was going on, these lads did what all lads did in school holidays. They mooched about, happy in each other's company. It did not matter that they had not got a rod between them. A bit of old line and a bent pin were all that were needed. Prized catches were stored in jam jars to be shown off later. 'If you think you're bringing that in here, you've another think coming,' was usually mum's greeting when they got home. Boys in short trousers were boys as God meant them to be. Knees were for grazing, not encasing in jeans from the moment a child could walk. The boy with his long trousers at half mast kept his school cap on, even in holiday time. No one thought it odd. He was proud of his school and his uniform. The canal they fished was the work of the 18th century engineer, James Brindley. As it passes Wedgwood's Etruria Works, the Trent and Mersey is 408 feet above sea level. When the young fishermen returned to school in September they looked higher than that. Over their heads the Battle of Britain would be fought.

The Warrillow Collection

The Warrillow Collection

Left: Can anything be more perfect than an English summer's day? For these children Etruria Woods was a place of magic. Fairy circles and pretty bluebells made it feel as if the town and potbanks were in a different land. It was a feast of butterflies and ladybirds. On the slopes bunnies ran free. Jays singing on the treetops and the hum of insects were the only sounds to disturb the peace and serenity of this idyllic scene. The children blew dandelion clocks and counted 'He loves me, he loves me not.' Daisies were picked in their scores. How carefully they were slit and wound in to decorative chains. The girls wore them around their necks as proudly as any princess with her string of pearls. The boys made dens and imagined they were in the jungle. They searched for buried treasure and then everyone joined in with a game of hide and seek. That disturbed the peaceful air, but no one ever objected to the sound of happy, carefree voices. There were many days like this in the summer of 1947. Long, hot and balmy days followed each other endlessly. When the parents brought the picnic they spread the sandwiches and buns on a blanket. Whilst the children tucked in and washed the food down with draughts of Tizer and fizzy lemonade the dads chatted about the marvellous feats of the Brylcreem boy, cricketer Denis Compton. That summer he scored more runs than anyone before or since. The mums wondered at Christian Dior's New Look and whether they would be able to keep up with the figure of eight shape that was now the in thing.

Above: Canals were an important part of the pottery industry. Even with the coming of the railway, many of the heavy raw materials it needed were moved on water. Laden coal barges were a familiar sight for local children. On 10 August 1960 the National Boat Rally was held on the Trent and Mersey canal. For a change, there were little sail boats, motor launches and prettily decorated houseboats to see, as well as the familiar barge. Feeding the swans was an added pleasure for this happy knot of nippers. Armed with crusts and stale bread, they happily fed the noble birds. They played games with them, teasing them playfully. Little titbits would be aimed in between two swans just to see them race to get there first. Carefully placed throws, each one getting nearer, were made to encourage the swans to come closer. The birds were crafty. They knew what the children were up to. They only came so close. In the background, Doulton Sanitary Potteries Ltd produced fittings for toilets in the homes the children came from. Industry was not all about Etruscan vases. There was the practical side as well. Whilst the wheels of industry turned, the children played on. Little sticks acted as pretend boats. They raced them through the water, but the calm waters of the canal meant that their progress was slow. Not that it mattered, it was just good fun.

Above: There will be no jokes about the initials on the front of the no 17 bus. They have been done to death. Potteries Motor Traction evolved from Potteries Electric Traction of the days when trams ran. The last of those left Hanley for Newcastle in 1928. The scooter parked at the kerbside was a common sight in 1967. This form of transport was popular with students and modernists. This was shortened to 'mods'. They collected music by the Small Faces, washed their hair and often wore long duffel coats. Their sworn enemies were the greasy bikers who still clung to the songs of Gene Vincent and Johnny Kidd. Known as 'rockers', they had connections with the later motorcycle gangs of Hell's Angels. In the 60s no bank holiday seemed complete without a pitched battle between the rival tribes. Clacton, Bournemouth and Brighton were just a few of the seaside resorts that put up the shutters when they heard the sound of two stroke engines coming into town. The film on at the Odeon would not have appealed to either group. 'Thoroughly Modern Millie' was an attempt to find another blockbuster for Julie Andrews. In 1964 she had starred in 'Mary Poppins' and followed it with another smash, 'The Sound of Music', the following year. This latest movie was not as successful, but still did well. The British singer and actress became Dame Julie Andrews in May 2000.

Below centre: The neon lights of the Odeon attracted cinema goers on Trinity Street like moths to a flame. The chain of Odeons was one of the most successful in Britain in those middle years of the 20th century. It is now 'The Foyer', but in 1959 it was showing the film version of one of the all time stage musical greats. To do the movie justice, the cinema was closed for two weeks so that special projection equipment could be fitted. Fred Woolley, the cinema's chief projectionist, took this photograph. He had also worked at the Gaumont. Fred was a dab hand, as he played the cinema organ as well. He would have enjoyed the music from 'South Pacific'. It contained some of the best loved songs of that or any era. As a Broadway show, in 1949 it ran for 2,000 performances. The Odeon brought the best of Hollywood to Hanley's movie buffs. Built on the site of the Grand, it was a must for a weekly visit. However, bingo and television combined to reduce cinema audiences to a trickle. By 1975, the decision to close its doors was made. The last film was shown on 15 November. That was also a musical. 'Tommy' was the final title appearing on the screen. 'Pinball wizard', though popular in its day, is not the sort of song that will be performed in future as often as 'Bali h'ai' or 'Happy talk'.

Below: The old museum on Pall Mall held a host of treasures. The schoolchildren on this visit passed examples from Packard and Ord, Pilkington, Richards and other names from the history of Potteries' tile making. What lay in store at the top of the grand staircase? Their young eyes were gazing hopefully upwards. We all have memories of our favourite educational visits. They usually followed the same pattern. Off we went to a museum or gallery armed with clipboards and pens. 'Miss' had given us our instructions in the classroom before we set off. There were worksheets to fill in and questions to answer. The next day we had to sit at our desks and try to remember what we had seen and learned. Some of us could only recall being told not to touch anything. Why put all that stuff out if you could not see what it felt like? Most of the children would rather have been on a visit to Chester Zoo. At least you could have a good laugh at the monkeys' bottoms. There was always ice cream and toffees on those trips. Crocodiles of kids, walking in twos, holding hands in case one escaped, and 'sir' telling Billy not to dawdle. It was worth wearing those silly labels round our necks to get out for the day. A working farm was best of all. There you could stroke the animals and wrinkle your nose at the smelly pigs.

Bottom: The mighty Ceramic City Choir is famous the length and breadth of the land. Performing for 60 years, it is an honour to be invited to join. Many a young tenor or budding soprano has been brokenhearted by not getting to join the its exalted ranks. But, quality knows no charity. A place earned is also one that is jealously guarded. Formed in the early years of the war, it provided an outlet for the members' interests away from the thoughts of battle. Audiences could get some escape from their everyday worries as they listened to the melodious sounds that rolled from the stage and over the stalls. It helped keep up our spirits during those gloomy times. The choir gave its first concert at the Victoria Hall in 1942. On one occasion, Queen Elizabeth II visited, looked at the mighty organ and said, 'It is the same make as mine!' Early on, Malcolm Sargent was a regular conductor. He was to lead London's Promenade Concerts from 1948 until his death in 1967. The top names in music were happy to be associated with the choir, such was its impressive reputation. John Barbirolli, conductor of Manchester's Hallé Orchestra for 25 years, was proud to come to our city to lead the Ceramic City Choir. In 1949 it was the turn of Adrian Boult to take the baton. The following year he would become the conductor of the London Philharmonic Orchestra. All three contemporary conductors were knighted for their services to music.

Spode - the royal potter

For almost two hundred and fifty years Spode china has been appreciated by both connoisseurs and ordinary people alike. Cups and saucers, plates and dishes bearing the Spode name are both treasured by collectors and also used throughout the world for daily meals. Yet when seven year old Josiah Spode was set to work for twelve hours a day in a pottery, the year after his father had died and been buried in a pauper's grave, no-one could have guessed that he was destined to make his name a household word in decades to come.

In 1749 when Josiah was 16 he took the first steps which would eventually lead him to fame and fortune. That year he was apprenticed to Thomas Whieldon who was at that time Staffordshire's most successful potter. Five years later, after serving his apprenticeship, and having reached the age of twenty-one and adulthood, Josiah moved on to work as a skilled potter for William Banks of Stoke but soon moved on to open his own small factory. Josiah began his own business making cream-coloured and blue-painted earthenware; his lines were obviously popular because he was eventually able to buy William Banks' factory from him; that site remains to this day the home of Spode. It was here that Josiah worked and experimented to find the best methods of making pottery and demonstrating a degree of determination and inventiveness which were in due course to pay a spectacular dividend.

Whilst Josiah Spode was developing his own skills, a great deal of experimentation with new ceramic materials was being carried out in the Potteries in the search for a material which could be used for the manufacture of white tableware. Chinese painted blue and white designs had been imported in quantity and had become popular but, since the East India Company had begun to reduce their imports

Above: *An illustration depicting Josiah Spode's first successful piece of fine bone china.*
Below: *The Spode Works 1833-4.*

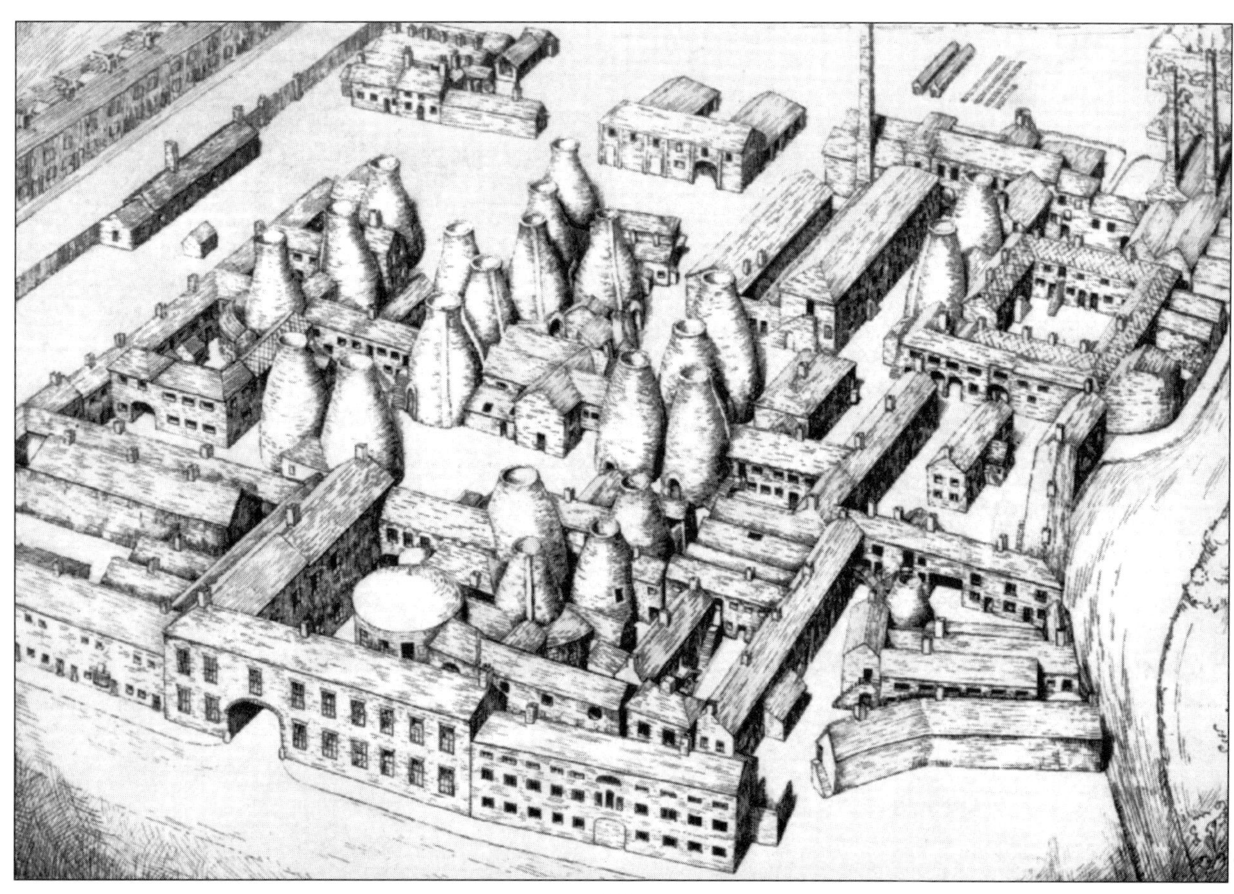

of chinaware in 1773, these items had become increasingly scarce. Potteries reproduced the Chinese designs by hand on the cream coloured ware of the time but could not produce them in sufficient quantity to meet demand. This was the time of the Industrial Revolution and a mechanised process was needed.

After much trial and error a process of blue underglaze printing on earthenware from hand-engraved copper plates was eventually perfected by Josiah Spode; that breakthrough established his reputation. By 1784 he had won wide acclaim for his achievement, and from then on the prosperity of his pottery was assured. But Josiah Spode was not content with that single achievement; he continued with his pioneering work, and in the closing years of the 18th century he was working to perfect the formula for making Fine Bone China.

Above: *A wartime royal visit by George VI and Queen Elizabeth.* ***Top:*** *King George V and Queen Mary visiting the Spode factory in 1913.* ***Right:*** *Prince Charles' visit on 2nd March 1998.*

All Spode ceramics are made in essentially the same way today as they were two hundred years ago. Since 1784, most blue and white ware has been transfer printed onto white earthenware. The Spode earthenware body is still made with the 1820 ingredients of calcined flint, china stone, china clay and ball clay. Designs are created initially on paper, then hand engraved onto copper plates; this is a highly-skilled process. The engraved plate is heated, then coated with metallic oxides mixed with oils, wiped clean of excess pigment and, after wetting with a solution of soap and water, a special tissue paper is laid on top. After passing through rollers to impress the paper onto the engraving, the tissue is peeled away to reveal the pattern printed in reverse. Cut out by hand, the printed tissue is carefully positioned before being rubbed down on the ware with a stiff brush. The whole piece is then immersed in running water until the tissue floats away, leaving the design on the ware.

Finally it is 'hardened on' in a kiln to remove the oils and leave only the metal oxides, before being glazed and fired to produce the rich, characteristic Spode blue, permanently protected under the glaze.

Josiah Spode's first designs created using his new process were reproductions of the Chinese porcelain designs and Chinese-style patterns. Other patterns soon followed, including the earliest blue florals. Three patterns originally introduced between 1790 and 1820 are still produced today: Blue Italian, Tower Blue and of course the immortal Willow pattern.

The original 18th century formula for its Fine Bone China is still used at the Spode factory. The raw ingredients are calcined bone, china clay and stone (china or Cornish). These are mixed with water in a 'blunger' before being purified and having a large proportion of the water removed in a filter press. After maturing for a few days, the clay passes through a pug mill to extract any air bubbles. 'Making' is divided into four main processes: flat making of plates, saucers, etc; cup making; pressing by hand of platters, and open vegetable dishes and casting, again by hand, or hollowware such as soup tureens, tea and coffee pots. The processes and techniques used at Spode today are essentially the same as those which Josiah Spode used, and, because the amount of mechanisation that can be employed in the manufacturing process is limited, a high degree of artistry, hand work and craftsmanship are required throughout all stages of production.

Above: *The Print Shop in 1926.*

Spode's formula for Fine Bone China was quite possibly the single most significant development in the history of the Potteries, as its brilliant whiteness and delicate translucency inspired new standards of artistry, skill and finish across the whole ceramics industry. There had been interest in the use of bone ash as a tableware ingredient from around 1750, and in fact it had been used in the middle ages in cupels for the assaying of metals. In the second half of the 18th century several experimental formulations were tried, but these were only 'soft-paste' porcelains with a little bone ash included. Evidence suggests that Josiah Spode was very close to perfecting his formula for bone china in the years before he died in 1797. Just how close he came we cannot be certain, but by 1799 his son, Josiah Spode II was successfully selling Spode's bone china.

Josiah Spode II had opened a showroom and a shop to sell his father's wares in Cripplegate in 1778. It was Josiah Spode II who was responsible for selling the company's products and by 1784 he had appointed another Staffordshire man, William Copeland, as the firm's first travelling sales representative. When the elder Josiah Spode perfected the process of blue underglaze printing in 1784, there was a ready market for these products because in that same year the tax on tea, which had previously been prohibitive, had been dramatically reduced. The tax cut led to an increase in the amount of tea which was drunk, which in turn led to an increase in the demand for teapots and tea services as more and more families became regular drinkers of tea, then perceived as a luxury drink with connotations of high social status. It seems probable that the Spodes had anticipated the tax changes and its consequences, and prepared themselves to take advantage of the expected growth in the market. The success of Spodes was assured by the combination of sound business sense, innovation and craftsmanship.

Above: *One of many designs (this one dating from 1853) from Spode's pattern book archive.*
Below: *Items from the Dressing Table and Toilet Service made for the use of HRH Princess Alexandra on the occasion of the presentation of the Freedom of the City of London to HRH The Prince of Wales in June 1863.*

Those visiting the Spode factory today can see pottery being created using essentially the same methods and techniques which Josiah Spode perfected in the late 18th century at the height of his creativity. The Spode tradition has always been one of innovation, however, and new techniques, particularly in the fields of quality control and firing, are continually explored and adopted provided that they are completely compatible with the Spode ethos.

Just as Josiah Spode responded to the needs of his day; so the company today remains closely in touch with customer's needs. Every year new patterns, decorations and special items are created, but always with the authentic Spode touch. There is a commitment to maintaining individual skills, flair and talent, creating distinctive shapes and decorations, and pursuing excellence rather than settling for what is simply convenient to mass produce.

Visitors can view Spode's collections of Fine Bone China and earthenwares including the Blue Room which is devoted entirely to elegant displays of blue Spode, showing over 300 antique items of the highest quality and beauty in a unique setting. Many of the designs will be familiar, and it is fascinating to discover just how far back their origins go - Blue Italian, for example, has been in continuous production since 1816 and is still popular today; whilst the first version of the Willow pattern plates were made by Spode around 1790.

Above: *Engraving copper plates.*
Left: *Some of the tools needed for engraving copper plates.* ***Top:*** *The entrance to the Spode Works.*

A visit to Spode is much more than an opportunity to see and appreciate the fascinating processes and time-honed craftsmanship that create works of outstanding beauty. It is also a living embodiment of one of the most important chapters in the history of ceramics.

The Visitor Centre offers a unique experience for all those who appreciate the world's finest Bone China and Imperial ware and who would like to know more about the oldest English pottery company still operating from the same historic site on which it was founded. The Visitor Centre, which is open seven days a week, offers the opportunity to view a video presentation of the history of Spode and of the ceramic industry, along with a Picture Gallery, Museum and Craft Demonstration Area. Those Craft Demonstrations include engraving, lithography, hand painting and clay casting can be simply watched or the more adventurous can even try out their own skills with Spode's 'Hands On Experience'.

The Museum at the Visitor Centre contains an unrivalled collection of exquisite ceramic masterpieces from the very beginnings in 1770, through the creative heydays of the 1800s, the patronage of the world's Royal households and the indulgences of the Empire all the way to the post-war era and modern times.

Visitors may join one of two fully guided tours around a true working factory, choosing from either the Basic Factory Tour or the Connoisseur Factory Tour.

***Above:** A production worker removing ware from a kiln. **Left:** One of the prestige hand painters. **Below:** Paper and copper plate going through the press.*

The Basic Factory Tour lasts approximately one and a half hours around the Factory site and provides an interesting and informative insight into over 200 years of tradition. The Connoisseur Factory Tour by contrast is an in-depth guided tour of approximately two and a half hours and includes the processes of manufacture and decoration, the Museum Gallery and the exclusive 'Blue Room' where early Spode 'Blue and White' ware dating from the 1780s is displayed on antique furniture. Those taking the Connoisseur Tour are also given refreshments in the Blue Italian Restaurant and a Connoisseur Pack as a memento of their visit.

On each of these tours highly qualified guides take visitors around the Factory to see skilled employees at their place of work. The guides explain all the processes that are involved in production from clay right through to the finished product and sales.

Unfortunately for disabled visitors, due to the antiquity of the site, wheelchair access is limited in certain areas and telephoning ahead is always advisable. The tours involve walking around the majority of the Factory site and some stairs are involved, therefore it may be unsuitable for persons who have difficulty in walking.

Above: *Father Christmas in his grotto.*
Top: *Part of Spode's annual World of Christmas.*
Left: *The world renowned Blue Room.*

Ironically children under 12 years old are not permitted on Factory Tours due to safety regulations, a development which would no doubt have pleased Josiah Spode given that he had worked in the industry since he had been little more than half that age!

Even though factory tours are not available at weekends the Visitor Centre still offers a great deal to interest, not least its factory shops which are open every day of the week. To produce the very best means that there will always be a percentage of pieces which do not meet the high standards of the final quality check even though their faults are hardly detectable; these items are put aside for sale at the most favourable prices exclusively from the on-site Factory Shops.

Also available is a comprehensive range of tabletop accessories, textiles and stationery in some of Spode's most famous patterns. Both national and international products are now also available from the many concession outlets at the Spode site.

The fully licensed 'Blue Italian Restaurant', is also open seven days a week to provide snacks, lunch, cream teas and quality refreshments, served on classic Blue & White tableware. This area is complemented by additional facilities, opened in 2000 as part of the ongoing development of the site, which are dedicated to the 'Willow Pattern'. Both areas are available for private bookings, including evenings and weekends.

Given the continuous development of the Spode site and the firm's commitment to developing new business opportunities it will come as no surprise to discover that Spodes now offers conference facilities to potential clients.

How proud Josiah Spode would have felt, had he guessed that tableware produced in his factory would continue to bring pleasure to so many generations, and that today, over two centuries later, craftsmen would still be making beautiful tableware in his factory, using the methods he developed. He would certainly have been proud to know that the quality standards he first set are being continued to this day. But more than just proud he would perhaps also be astonished to find that the small firm which he, a humble pauper's son, began all those years ago today carries on its letterhead that ultimate accolade for a British firm, the words: 'By Appointment to Her Majesty Queen Elizabeth II Manufacturer of China - Spode Stoke-on-Trent'.

Above centre: *One of the conference rooms.*
Top left: *The Blue Italian Restaurant.*
Top right: *The Balmoral Queen Mother's Anniversary Vase.* ***Left:*** *One of the factory shops.*

The Warrillow Collection

Scenes from the sky

The war years were fairly kind to Stoke-on-Trent, by comparison, anyway. Luftwaffe bombers headed for Birmingham and Coventry, or north to Liverpool and Manchester. Although there were some raids, the city did not suffer in the way that others did. This photograph was taken when the balance of the war was still delicately poised. It is a 1943 scene, looking across towards Shelton. Below is Etruria. The neatly laid out houses were all similar to each other. In the blackout it must have been hard to tell one from another. This district had once been home to the Josiah Wedgwood pottery factory. When this photograph was taken, the factory had only recently moved to new premises at Barlaston. Many of the pottery workers would still have lived on this estate, though there were plenty of other potteries nearby if they wanted to work nearer home. Wedgwood and Joseph Pickford, the designer of the 1769 Etruria Works, had coined the fanciful name of this part of Stoke-on-Trent. Pickford was also the architect for the Wedgwood family home, Etruria Hall. Wedgwood chose the name because of the Italian style of classical pottery he produced. The Etruscans were a member of the ancient people of Etruria in a part of Italy between the Tiber and Arno rivers, west and south of the Apennines. Their urban civilisation reached its height in the sixth century B.C. The Romans, their successors to power in the peninsula, adopted many features of Etruscan culture. Wedgwood was fascinated with the Etruscan wall frescoes and realistic terracotta portraits found in their tombs.

This aerial view of Hanley shows Broad Street entering the picture at the bottom left. It runs to the junction with Bethesda Street, where Broad Street becomes Piccadilly. That, in turn, runs north towards where the Potteries shopping centre now stands. The housing at the bottom right has all gone, making way for Hanley Library. Thc sitc of Bell Pottery has taken on a new significance. The works and bottle ovens were knocked down to make way for the City Museum and Art Gallery that moved here from Pall Mall in 1956. On the opposite side of the street from Bell Pottery the distinctive curve of Bethesda Chapel can be clearly seen. It was to become derelict, but, at its height, it boasted a congregation of 2,000. Its associated school is to the chapel's right. Continuing up the right hand side of the photograph, from the school, the edge of the Town Hall, Tontine Market and the Post Office can be made out. The parish church of St John's was once a fine and attractive grade II listed building. It can be seen top centre. When its tower was declared unsafe, the church was closed in 1985. Bodies in the graveyard were exhumed as Potteries Way, the A50 ring road, was built in the 1980s. The distant slag heaps and waste tips were reclaimed in the 1960s and 1970s and turned into parkland.

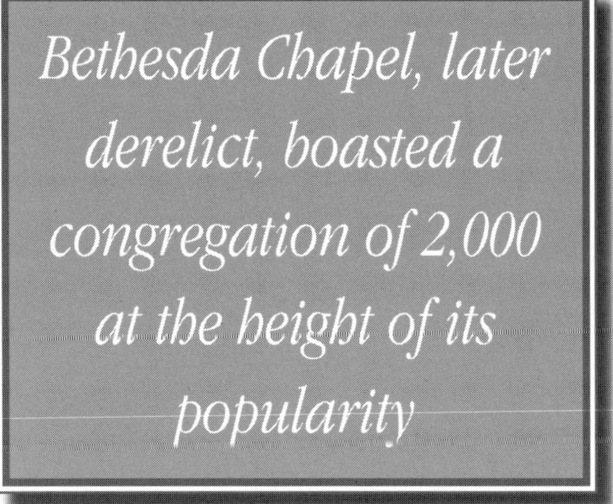

This stunning aerial view of Hanley was taken in the late 1950s. Looking north across the town, there are many landmarks that the famous son of Hanley, Sir Stanley Matthews, would have recognised. Soccer's first footballing knight was born in Seymour Street on 1 February 1915, not far from the Caldon Canal, to the east of the photograph. He would have recalled many of the sights that have now changed forever. Broad Street comes into view at the bottom as it turns past Swinnerton's. The factory grew around the bottle ovens, so that only their chimneys looked out above the rooftop. College Road runs off to the right towards Stoke station. The entrance to Shelton Church, St Mark's, is opposite the Victoria Pottery.

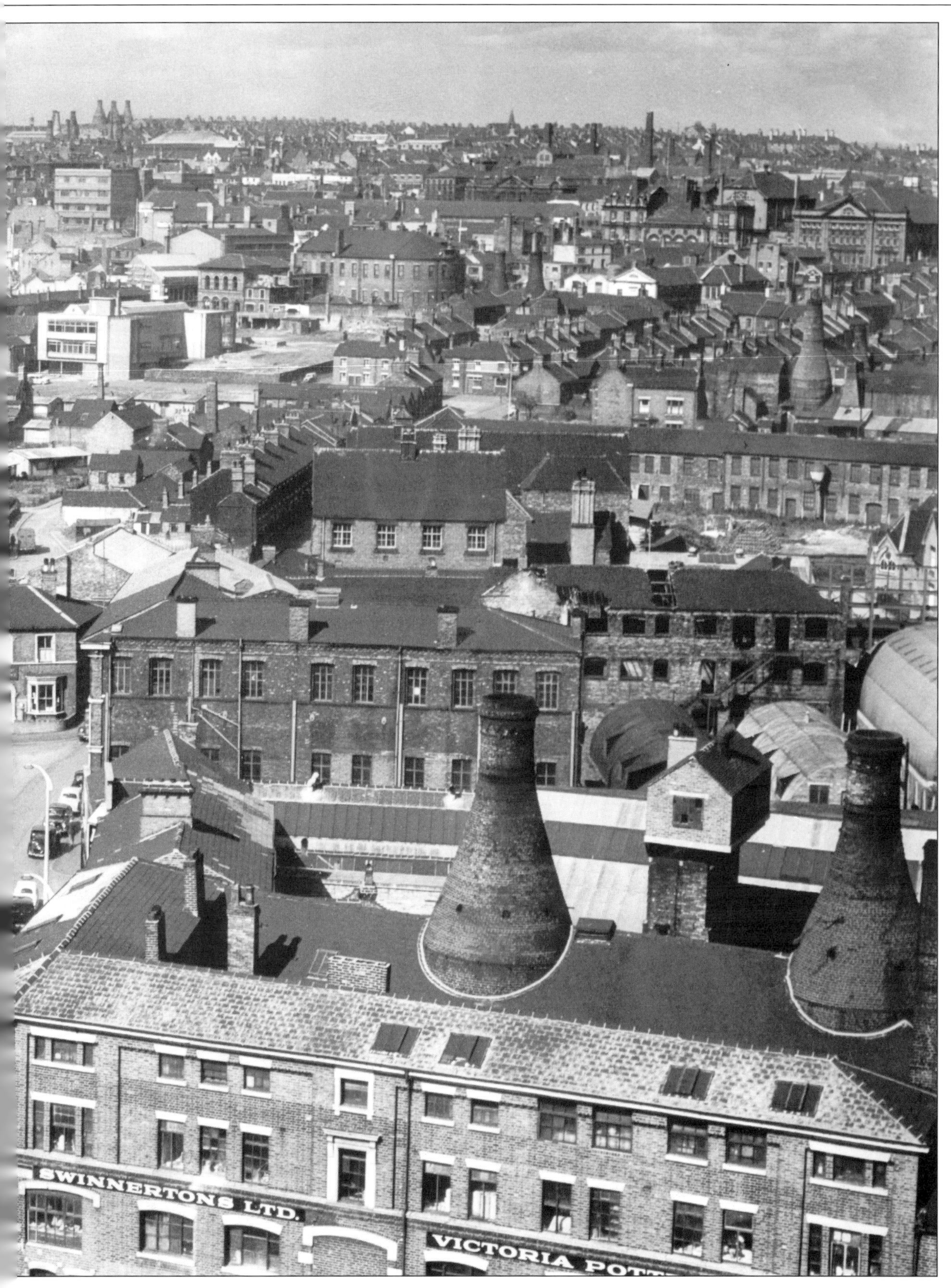

Evans Halshaw's garage later commanded most of the old factory area. Much of the scene is now greatly changed. At the top left, beyond where the prefabs stood, the Potteries Shopping Centre is now dominant. Further beyond, the wasteland of Hanley Deep Pit has been reclaimed and turned into Central Forest Park. The redundant St John's Church is in the centre of the skyline. Still standing, it is an example of a steel framed building, but has fallen into disrepair. Landmarks for the 21st century include the new museum, top centre. The distinctive rounded shape of the old Bethesda Chapel is just beyond it. Other buildings of note are at the top right and include the Town Hall, Post Office and Victoria Hall. Sir Stan is also just a memory. The grand old man died in 2000.

The rooftops of Stoke, with the inevitable smoke filled skies beyond, are the focus of this 1947 photograph. Stoke-on-Trent was an agricultural area until the end of the 18th century. It is fitting, with such a history, that it was chosen to host the National Garden Festival in 1986. The centre of the festival was placed around the old site of Wedgwood's Etruria at what has now been developed into Festival Park. The name of Stoke is thought to come for the old English word for a holy place. Religious links to Cistercian monks who settled in the area in medieval times can be traced. The connection with the area and 18th and 19th century Methodism is well known. But, until the days when the Industrial Revolution made its impact, there was little to Stoke other than one church and a few scattered dwellings. The church we can see today dates from the 1820s. What remained of the 13th century building was erected once again in 1887 and sited close by the present church. It was the development of the turnpike from Newcastle to Derby and the opening of the Trent and Mersey Canal that kickstarted life into Stoke. By the Victorian age the town had largely taken the shape we can now see. There are now some 25,000 inhabitants in an area that was home to just a few dozen little more than two centuries ago.

Stoke was an agricultural area until the end of the eighteenth century

The Warrillow Collection

Memorable moments

Thankfully this is not the Hanley branch of the Hitler Youth in training for its next assault on humanity! In a scene reminiscent of those fitness and beauty exercises of yesteryear, local youngsters are playing their part in the Wedgwood Pageant. In 1930, to celebrate the 200th anniversary of the birth of Josiah Wedgwood, Hanley Park became the centre for the celebrations. There was plenty to recall and give thanks for. Wedgwood and his fellow potters had provided work for the residents and development for the region since the middle of the 18th century. People turned out in their thousands to mark their appreciation of the Potteries' unique way of life. But it was not an event limited to local residents. People booked train tickets and boarded 'charas' from far and wide to join in the fun. The travel agent, Thomas Cook, advertised the event nationally and the floodgates opened. The pageant ran for a full week in May. Every new day saw a different chapter in history being acted out. The carnival kicked off with the Druids and, all through the week, a cast of 5,000 acted out historical scenes. In celebration of local industry there just had to be a pottery tableau included. About 1,500 local workers made it a tableau to be remembered. The entertainment went on late into the evenings with a military tattoo, dancing, fireworks, concerts and a torchlight display. The children's gymnastics display that you are looking at had 3,000 youngsters participating.

The Warrillow Collection

Right: People crowd the streets whenever a royal visitor comes to call. Then, cheering hordes wave to the dignitaries in the black limousines that slide past. There was no such merriment this day in 1952. The crowd was made up of journalists, typesetters, sub editors, proofreaders and all the other employees who went to make up the staff of the Sentinel. The occasion was a sad one. The limo was the hearse that carried the coffin of EN Scott. He was the much respected editor of Stoke-on-Trent's mighty newspaper. Friends, family and colleagues mourned his passing. The regard in which his staff held him is well illustrated in the turn out on the Sentinel steps. The newspaper has been around since 1854. It reported on a very different age when it was launched. Born as the Staffordshire Sentinel and Commercial and General Adviser, it must have cost a fortune in ink just to set up the name at the paper's head! The paper entered Victorian life without the computer aided technologies available to the press of today. There were no telephones, cars or electrical aids. Some news was gathered by cable. Otherwise, cub reporters scurried off on foot and filed their copy by whatever means they could. Even carrier pigeon service was used to get a story from the notebook to the newsdesk. The Sentinel office had a special pigeon tower. Carriers, with tiny little baskets on their legs, flew the tale of a rail crash or prize marrow across the skies to this unique cote.

Below: Rag Week at Keele in the early 1960s and the students were having fun. Quite what the departed spirit of poor Leo had done to deserve his fate remains shrouded in mystery. Keele 'Karnival' was a time of high spirits. Students kidnapped dignitaries and held them to ransom. They produced little books of smutty jokes you were forced to buy. Our brainy sons and daughters then got sloshed. Mostly we forgave them. The money raised by their japes all went to charitable causes. Around the time of this photograph, the University College of North Staffs was officially becoming the University of Keele. It now has a fine reputation and a good balance of traditional buildings mixed in with the new. When the College first opened lectures took place in Nissen huts! As the float passed Burton's sports and angling shop, the billboards proclaimed the slogans and products of the day. Hartley's peas were fresh from the garden, so we were told. Stergene bleach was a popular product to pour down the toilet and Omo brightness was something we just had to have. Other washing powders of the day included Tide, Oxydol and Rinso. The Daz challenge was going even then. Pop singer Craig Douglas promoted it and the old crooner Jimmy Young urged us to get Flash. The students took more notice of Ansell's, 'the better beer'. They had their priorities right.

The Warrillow Collection

Above: This happy band of workers was looking forward to what was to grow on this site. It was to be the home of the new Wedgwood village at Barlaston, just south of Stoke-on-Trent. Ever since 1930 plans had been laid to move the Wedgwood factory from Etruria to Barlaston. Mining subsidence meant that the old place was threatening to sink into the workings and so an estate was purchased here. Production moved to the new site in 1940. The war restricted development as energies were channelled elsewhere. It was a different matter in peace-time. Output and development increased and, by 1950, Barlaston was handling the whole lot. The fashion statement these ladies were making is interesting. Over half a century ago no woman would be seen without her handbag. All manner of compacts, hankies, lipsticks and purses were hidden away inside. Even when trekking across a muddy field, that necessary accessory was firmly clutched. The young woman in the ankle socks would have been one of the first of Britain's bobbysoxers. The term that came over from America was soon applied to any adolescent girl. It was particularly used to describe those who swooned at crooners like Frank Sinatra.

Top: This is a good snap. That could mean the photo or the food. Miners took their food underground in special tins that kept food fresh and dry. It also kept out the rats. Many other workers used the term 'snap' to refer to their food, but it was the miners who really coined it. The Kemball Training Centre at Mount Pleasant, Fenton provided young lads fresh from school with the necessary knowledge. They learnt all about drilling techniques. Just as important were lectures on health and safety. Despite that, in 1950, outside the centre, the trainees were wearing safety hats made of compressed cardboard. Ernest Bevin, the first leader of the Transport and General Workers' Union, was Minister of Labour during the war. In 1943 'Bevin boys' were called up and conscripted to work the pits. The pictured lads chose to work in a training scheme begun in 1946. At the time, there were 15,000 employed in local collieries. Coal was one of the major industries. Rich seams provided ready fuel for the growing pottery businesses in the late 18th century. As the potbanks grew, so did the number of mines. By the second half of the 20th century, competition from overseas and the introduction of gas-fired kilns caused the coal industry to struggle. A year-long strike in the 1980s helped band people together, but had little effect on the further decline in the industry.

Above: Christmas decorations and party time was soon to be with them. Before then, there was a job to be done. There was a war to be won. Battles were fought overseas, but there was an army of essential workers to be fed at home. During World War II the wheels of industry had to keep turning. Food to feed the stomach of heavy industry was provided by the canteen girls at Swinnerton's factory on Gower Street, Cobridge. Dressed in their clean, hygienic overalls, with the pert little caps on their heads, they were surrounded by mounds of bread. 'Workers' Playtime', broadcast on the Light Programme, blared out of tannoys overhead. Popular singers and comedians performed in works' canteens up and down the country. Their efforts kept spirits high. The entertainment was relayed to homes and factories across the nation. All the while, knives flew and marge was spread on slice after slice. The butties the Swinnerton girls made were known as 'miners' sandwiches'. Others in heavy industry were also supplied, but it was the underground workers who were the main customers. For just 4d (less than 2p today), two rounds of sandwiches, or one and a piece of fruit cake, were on their way to the snap boxes. The fillings were also a special treat. Sometimes there was boiled ham. That was something. In the shops, you could not get it for love or money.

Right: The restaurant at Trentham Gardens, that later became the Roman Bar, in 1942 was the centre of wartime activity. Even during hostilities there had to be a refreshment break. These women had earned their cuppa. Most had come up from London to work in the finance clearing banks that had been set up in Trentham Gardens. Whilst shells were being fired, there were still the shillings to be looked after. Keeping the finances of the country going was just as crucial to the war effort as digging for victory or joining the ARP. A lot of the women were anxious about leaving their homes and coming north. It was understandable. In those days north of Watford was a foreign land. But, they were pleased with the welcome they were given. Local women and, as you might expect, a lot of the men, made them feel at home. Lifelong friendships were born. After the war was over, Christmas cards, regular letters and visits helped new friends become old ones. Some of the women never went back. They settled in the area, having found a life that suited them better than the one down south. In the years that followed, others returned to the Potteries. They missed the friends they had made so much. Every cloud has a silver lining. Even the dark days of the war brought a togetherness that is endearingly British. Hitler won some battles, but he lost the war. He just could not break down the bonds that tied Britons together.

Left: Don't you just love them? Little cherubs, one and all. Faces of pure innocence that warm the cockles of your heart. What a pity they could not stay like that for all time. At least in the world of photography, it was possible. This picture of the Broom Street School Christmas party is frozen in time. Those faces will never get any older or be affected by the pains of adolescence or the wrinkles of old age. The school is near what is now Central Forest Park, Hanley. In the 1950s these children and their mums and teachers did not worry a jot about the little ones' progress. They knew they would learn to read and write, do their sums and be happy wee souls. No National Curriculum, no Ofsted inspectors and no complicated lesson plans to get in the way of being kids. They succeeded without those. On the day that their party was taking place, the children were surrounded by what they really needed - caring adults. Buns had been baked, biscuits bought and sandwiches carefully cut and spread from the meagre ration allowance. Orangeade was abundant and angelic faces would soon have been smeared with jam and juice. Party hats had been carefully put together in craft lessons and the adults joined in the fun. Sometimes you wondered if they had even more jollity than the pupils did. Where are the Broom Street children now? Are they as happy as grown ups, or do they recall what really were the best days of their lives?

Above: This part of the city centre is now pedestrianised. The picture was taken from what is now the Potteries Shopping Centre. A statue to England's most famous footballer, Sir Stanley Matthews, now stands in the centre of the road, to the right. The union flags flying from the shop windows suggest that this might have been around the time of Queen Elizabeth's coronation. It was always a busy part of Hanley. Three major stores stood side by side. Some modernisation has taken place since, but they still serve the same purpose half a century later. Marks and Spencer always provided the shopper with good quality and sensible clothing. Its range of St Michael goods was quite enough for the vast majority of women in the 50s. Flashy boutiques and their trendy music were over a decade away. The new school year was about to start. Pleated skirts and green PE knickers had to be chosen. The skirts had to be of regulation length. They had to pass the kneeling test. If you went on your knees, the hem had to touch the floor. The lads needed short, grey trousers until they reached a certain age. The rules took no account of some lanky youths looking like giraffes in shorts. Next door was 'Woolies'. The original 'nothing over sixpence' store seemed to attract the doziest of shop assistants in those days. When you went to the counter with a purchase they always seemed to say, 'How much is it, love?'

Choirs grew from the ranks of those in the stalls and pews of the churches. Heavily influenced by Methodism, their first official outings in the 19th century drew on a repertoire of hymns and uplifting songs. Salvation Army bands continued the religious links. As the prissy Victorian age closed, choirs like the Madrigal Society were widening their appeal. Local bands started to gain a reputation. Around 1900, the White Cliff band was one of the best known. Collieries had their own brass bands and they marched and paraded proudly at festivals and on the Whit walks. The Ceramic City Choir continued the fine musical tradition. Formed during World War II, it did not take long to thrill local audiences with the quality of its music. As fame spread, the choir was invited to perform at major venues all over the country. Its massed ranks were in London after the war, playing to yet another packed house. The choir took time off from rehearsals to do a little sight seeing. The musicians have been photographed on the terrace of the Houses of Parliament. If they had gone inside they would have heard debate rage about interesting topics. These included the groundnuts scheme, the American publication of the memoirs of 'Crawfie' (the royal nanny) and a report from the Annual Abstract of Statistics. Despite missing out on those riveting topics, the choir still enjoyed visiting the Tower of London, Buckingham Palace and Madame Tussaud's.

The Warrillow Collection

On the home front

In 1940, with enough petrol coupons for your car, you could sweep along the road from Hanley and Burslem to this fine hotel, the Sneyd Arms, protected here by an array of sandbags. Tunstall was proud of this fine building. Its very name reminded residents of the historic traditions of the Potteries. The town claims to be the oldest of the six towns. The Audley and Sneyd families were born of Norman stock. Their ancestors were the first of William the Conqueror's Norman Lords of Stafford. The two families established the manor at Tunstall in the 13th century and successive generations were to become lords of the manor. Ralph Sneyd was one such person and a descendant of his, the Reverend W Sneyd, laid part of the gardens at Keele Hall, now a part of the university. Burslem residents have long disputed Tunstall's claim to seniority, but you would never have been able to convince a regular at the Sneyd Arms of anything else. The family name lives on in the names of streets and places across the county. There is an avenue, a crescent and a terrace in Newcastle bearing the family name. Even Leek has a street and an avenue. There is Sneyd Place, just off the Tunstall Western Bypass and Sneyd Street in Cobridge. Of course, there is Sneyd Hill Park, Sneyd Green and the Sneyd Trading Estate. Once there was Sneyd Colliery. All these act as permanent reminders of the days when we peasants touched our forelocks to the mighty lords of Tunstall Manor.

Below: She does not look very natty. So what? Appearances were not important. She had a job to do. Without her efforts, and those of millions of other women, the men would not have anything to return to. She was one of the women who kept the country on its feet during World War II. A member of the Women's Land Army, she had her boots on to do a special job. She was helping maintain the grounds in Hanley Park. It was not just flowers and shrubbery that she tended, but vegetable beds to provide extra food for the population that was blockaded by the U boats. Merchant shipping was struggling to get through and we had to rely on growing a lot of our own produce. Out in the fields, women drove tractors, forked hay and raised the livestock. Many girls in the Land Army had come from the cities. Billeted in rural villages and on farms, they soon found out that country life was tough. Delicate hands grew callouses and backs ached from forking and lifting. It was hard, but they did it. The men had gone off to war and the women made sure that the land was fit for their return. A new breed of woman emerged from those times. 'Women's work' now included agriculture, mechanics and industrial labour. The so called weaker sex proved what it knew all along. It was more than a match for mere men.

Right: Pottering on an allotment gives great pleasure to the amateur gardener and can help the weekly budget go a bit further. It also helps get men out from under women's feet. It was a popular hobby for the mining community. After hours underground it was marvellous to get out in the fresh air. The annual horticultural show in Hanley was the target for many of the keener gardeners. They lavished affection on marrows and onions. Special treatment and lots of TLC led to prize specimens and prize rosettes at the show. But, the pottering stopped in 1939. The men went off to war. The land girls moved in. Growing food became a necessity, not a hobby. These members of the Women's Land Army were maintaining the gardens in Hanley Park. The Dig for Victory campaign encouraged the public to become green fingered overnight. Every available piece of space was turned over to cultivation. Parks became huge allotments. Open spaces were planted out and even roadside verges became beds for lettuces and cabbages. Although it was mainly young women who joined the Land Army, older housewives did not shirk their responsibilities. They ran the home and worked in the factories. In their so called spare time, they bent their backs and tilled the land. The Civil Defence and the volunteer brigades were the armies that Hitler could not defeat.

Left: It was thought that this photograph was taken c1943, but the cadets' shoes look more modern than that. Either they were ahead of their time or they had been beamed into a different time zone. Perhaps their boots had been packed away in their baggage. If these were members of 237 Squadron of the Air Training Corps (ATC), they would need stronger footwear. On their way to Stoke station, it would have been the training camp that was beckoning them to go on manoeuvres. The ATC acted as a training ground for the Royal Air Force. During the second world war many young men were rushed into cockpits of fighter planes with only the most basic of training. The loss of life in the battle to keep our skies safe meant that those who were little more than boys had to grow up overnight. Today, the ATC is no longer a recruiting arm of the RAF, though many go on to careers in the services. The Corps' aim now is to promote a practical interest in aviation and to foster a spirit of adventure. It is open to young men and women between the ages of 13 and 18. There are 10,000 female cadets among the 38,000 cadets. Famous names who were once members include the former world light heavyweight boxing champion, John Conteh, and Sir Brian Rix, the actor and charity worker. The Duke of Edinburgh is the proud Air Commodore-in-Chief.

Above: Light tanks came rolling down Parliament Row, Hanley in 1941. Happily, they were not Panzers. Those divisions had been the main thrust of the German invasion of Poland in 1939. The Netherlands, Belgium, Luxembourg and France in 1940 all heard the rumble of the caterpillar tracks as they fell under the Nazi onslaught. In the campaign against France, there were 10 Panzer divisions involved. There were 2,574 German tanks in that campaign, out of the 3,400 tanks that Germany possessed. The cobblestones of the city centre shook as shoppers stood and watched the parade drive by. The army was on a morale and fund raising exercise. Special tank, warship and aeroplane weeks were to become regular efforts in the 1940s. Rather than just ask for money, the government used the idea first tried successfully in the 1914-18 war. Towns and cities focused on raising funds for a single purpose. People could then identify with the aim. One week it would be funding for a battleship, the next for a Spitfire. That went down well with locals. Stoke-on-Trent's own Reginald Mitchell was the plane's designer. Towns were encouraged to compete with neighbours to see which ones would top the fund raising league table. Thermometers, charting the progress, appeared on town halls and in market places. Aluminium saucepans were handed in and reappeared flying through the skies, bearing the roundels of the RAF.

The Warrillow Collection

Time in motion

Above: Looking across from Queen's Hall, the camera has been pointed in the direction of Burslem Town Hall. At just after noon on a day in 1956, there is plenty of evidence that the good times are returning to the country. There might have been a crisis in Suez, but the government was telling us that everything was under control and we did seem to have more in our wage packets. There were more goods to spend our spare cash on and the motor car was no longer the great luxury it once had been. The Town Hall had been looking down on this scene since the days of the pony and trap. It originally dated from 1761. That was when the lords of the manor granted land for the building of a market hall. This acted as the focus for all those from the outlying rural communities when they came to sell their wares and to barter for or buy goods in return. As it was the established centre, it was only natural that, when the hall was demolished in 1854, the replacement building became the centre of administration. Officially opened in 1857 and built at a cost of £10,000 to an Italian Renaissance style designed by GT Robinson, it is famous for its gilded angel. Sitting high on the rooftop, this winged figure came to represent civic victory. The clock tower, with its gas lit dial, was remodelled in 1925. A new mechanism was put in place, though the bell was retained.

Above right: A whole fleet of Potteries' coaches, packed with several hundred youngsters, is ready to roll off down the road. We are not told about the trip, but it was probably one made in the 1950s. Those children will be well into middle age by now. They might have come from one of the new estates that appeared. There had been a drive to put up low cost, but quality, housing. The Sutton Housing Trust was one of the agencies involved. The estates were places where many of us grew up. But, it was special days out that are best remembered. Pity the poor coach driver's ears as he steered his 'chara' towards the North Wales resorts of Rhyl, Prestatyn or Colwyn Bay. The excited chatter of children rose to fever pith, the closer he got. If he took the road through Queensferry there was enough frustration to stretch his frayed nerves even more. The traffic jams at that bottleneck were a daily occurrence during the holiday period. The children did not worry. They knew that sandcastles, looking for crabs in rock pools and beach cricket was waiting for them. Ice creams, dripping with raspberry juice, and a fish and chip supper on the way back; life was so simple and such fun. At least the driver got three cheers at the end.

Travel links with the outside world

In the 18th century, whilst the Americans were leading up to their War of Independence and events across the Channel were laying the foundations for what would be the French Revolution, the Potteries, as it would become known, was cut off from the rest of the world. As a largely rural place, with some local cottage industry in earthenware, locals had little need of travel. The area was landlocked. Rivers were not properly navigable and major roads passed it by. When Josiah Wedgwood and his fellows started to produce goods on a large scale they had major problems bringing in large amounts of raw material. They could not easily move large quantities of fragile pottery any distance, so marketing was a problem. Road links with the outside world were little more than packhorse trails. In 1759 Wedgwood was the prime mover behind the opening of the first turnpike roads in the area. The Derby-Uttoxeter-Newcastle road gave him the outlet he needed. Soon there were turnpikes all over the Potteries. Today's Newcastle to Leek road is one legacy of that era. However, it took until about 1814 for regular stage and mail coaches to pass through the centre of the district.

Still Wedgwood was not content. He wanted further means of moving his products. Enter James Brindley. A Derbyshire man, trained as a millwright, he had been working as an engineer in the Lancashire coalfields. In 1759 the Duke of Bridgwater hired him to build a canal from Worsley to Manchester so that the Duke's coal could be moved ready for wider distribution. Wedgwood recognised Brindley's ability and encouraged him to build a canal from Runcorn through Burslem and Stone. On 26 July 1776, Josiah Wedgwood cut the first sod for the Trent and Mersey Canal, but without Brindley. He had died four years earlier. The 700 foot rise at Harecastle was no problem. He drove a tunnel through the hillside. When the railway steamed into life in the mid 1800s, further change was on the way. The new wonder of the day gave quick and easy access for both goods and people to the rest of the country. In the Potteries rail travel developed from the horse drawn trams on railways around Bignall Hill and Partridge Nest. These early tracks provided a link between places of manufacture and a land sale wharf. The opening of North Staffordshire Railway (NSR) in 1849 gave access to the national network. Local lines flourished, but had competition from trams that began running, firstly along Waterloo Road in 1861. By 1905 there was a spider's web of overhead wires and cables running across from Meir to Goldenhill as the trams became electrified. Further competition was on hand from the internal combustion engine. The very first Potteries Motor Show of any size was held in 1907. The tram system declined and motorised buses and private cars replaced the old clanking contraptions. The 'Knotty', as the NSR was affectionately known, was swallowed up by LMS in 1923.

The 20th century saw a rise in road travel. The M6 motorway came to Staffordshire in 1963. The A34, the old Carlisle-London highway, became a dual carriageway in the 1960s and Queensway, the link to the motorway, appeared in the 1970s. Further remodelling of ring roads and the restyling of the A50 road to Derby helped change the pace of life in the Potteries. The closure of many small railway lines and stations under Dr Beeching's axe in the 1960s changed many of our travelling patterns. Passenger services from Stoke to Leek to Uttoxeter, from Cresswell to Cheadle and the loop lines from Etruria to Kidsgrove and Stoke to Silverdale were all affected. We said goodbye to stations at Fenton, Normacot, Mow Cop, Radway Green and Meir. All in the name of progress, we were told.

As roads become more clogged, 21st century gridlock seems a distinct possibility. Perhaps we ought to take to the houseboat and drift off along the Trent and Mersey, following the ghosts of Brindley and Thomas Telford through the Harecastle tunnels.

Driving forces

All of us have seen lorries bearing the name A & H Davey with their distinctive red, white and blue livery, but who were A & H Davey? Those who know the firm's ERF trucks may wonder too about A & H Davey's relationship with its sister company, Beech's Garage, a firm whose name has become synonymous with ERF throughout the road haulage industry.

A & H Davey (Roadways) Ltd

A & H Davey (Roadways) Ltd was founded by the husband and wife team of Arthur and Hilda Davey in 1944. Before and during the second world war, prior to striking out on his own, Arthur Davey had managed his father's Stoke and London-based haulage business, A E Davey & Sons.

The new general haulage company began life in Wolstanton housed in a large corrugated iron shed just large enough for two or three vehicles.

Despite most things, including fuel, being rationed the firm's founders had the foresight to start their company just as allied victory in the second world war began to seem possible. Arthur Davey sold his car to buy his first lorry - and bought a bicycle to travel to and from work.

The business used its original premises in Wolstanton from 1944 until the nationalisation of road haulage in 1949. As a result of nationalisation the firm diversified and bought two coaches. In the early 1950s trips were organised to the Festival of Britain in London, seaside resorts and further afield to Spain and Portugal. Arthur also went into partnership with another haulage company operating un-nationalised tippers working within a radius of fifty miles from a base in Hanley.

Around 1953 when it was decided to de-nationalise the industry Arthur was one of the first in North Staffordshire to go back into long distance haulage. To acquire a haulage firm one had to tender for vehicles being disposed of by British Road Services.

Above: *Company founder Arthur Davey.* ***Below:*** *1958 KV Cab 4 Wheeler 44G. 8 ton carrying capacity. Complete with sideboards ready for loading loose flints from Shoreham and Dartford for the pottery industry.*

before 'retiring' following her marriage and starting a family.

In the years following Arthur Davey's death the business continued to grow. The company's premises were very small and when the opportunity arose the family bought the adjoining premises and their garage became four times larger.

Eventually however the premises were acquired by the local authority when the land was needed for a new road (the A500 or D Road as it is known locally). In 1969 a new purpose built garage and offices were built - 10,000 sq ft - for the repair and maintenance of the fleet of vehicles which had now grown to 50 articulated tractors and around 90 trailers. A 45,000 sq ft warehouse was also built alongside the garage and offices.

If the tender was accepted you were in business - and Arthur Davey's bid was accepted: his first purchase was a 5x6 tonnes Thornycrofts. As soon as he was able he began to modernise the fleet of diesel trucks buying ERF trucks manufactured in Sandbach some 15 minutes away from the depot.

The company started to build a customer base and by 1956 had acquired eight vehicles. Sadly that year Arthur died aged just 44 years.

Hilda Davey kept the company going with the help of her son Barry and daughter Kathleen. Barry who was a student apprentice at Foden Motor Works at Elworth at the time left his apprenticeship to join the company. Barry ran the transport operation and his sister Kathleen looked after the accounts

In 1983 A & H Davey (Roadways) Limited bought the local ERF distributor Beech's Garage (1983) Limited. The reasoning behind this was that the Davey's fleet of vehicles were all ERFs and it made sense to consolidate the two companies.

Top: *1960 Motor Show at Earls Court, London. 8 x 4 24 ton gross - 15 ton carrying capacity. New 150 Gardner Engine with disc brakes.*
Above: *New C15 1950 ready for loading tyres from Michelin Tyre Co Stoke.*

Historically A E Davey's fleet had also consisted of ERF 5-14 ton gross lorries - the first vehicle A E Davey had bought in 1933 had been an ERF in ERF's first year of production.

In 1995 it made sense to find a site large enough to house both companies and it is from that site in Shelton New Road, Cliffe Vale Stoke-on-Trent that the two businesses are now run.

Today Davey's lorries regularly run between Stoke-on-Trent and Manchester, Liverpool, London, Brighton, Ramsgate and all of the south coast.

The business has retained many of its customers for over fifty years. Current customers include Michelin Tyres of Stoke-on-Trent and Eternit Building Materials (originally G H Downings) of Madeley Heath. Eternit manufacture clay tiles, a product which needs very specialised equipment to off load; for that business Davey's uses crane-mounted rigid vehicles, crane-mounted articulated vehicles and trailer-mounted (transportable) fork-lift trucks attached to the rear of vehicles. In order to service Imerys (formerly English China Clay) in Stoke-on-Trent the company also has specialist vehicles which enable it to discharge loose clay into smaller manufacturing units.

Company Chairman Barry Davey is proud of the fact that they are one of the oldest established haulage companies in North Staffordshire and whether it is one roof tile to a building site, a single tyre to a distributor or a 24 tonne sectional building to a site they pride themselves on next day delivery. The firm is built on service and customer relationships: and the customer comes first.

Their technical superiority is based on flexibility using specialised equipment and a full range of different types of vehicle for carrying building materials such as roofing tiles and bricks with crane and forklift offloading, tippers, super cube tautliners, low loaders, coil carriers for steel and vehicles for carrying loose clay for the pottery industry.

As their customers grow so will A & H Davey (Roadways) Limited. As a service provider they are only too pleased to add to the many different types of vehicles that they already have to fulfil the needs of their customers.

Three generations of the family have now been involved in Arthur and Hilda's company. The company is currently run by their son Barry Davey. Barry's son Ashley joined the business in 1995 after completing an engineering degree.

We wonder what Arthur Davey's thoughts might be if he were to see the size of the modern fleet of vehicles which have emerged from the proceeds of the sale of his car in 1944. Would he have thought it was worth cycling to work all those years ago?

Above: *A new 1937 ERF Type IV 9 ton vehicle. Carrying capacity 6 ton with LK Gardner Engine.*

Beech's Garage (1983) Ltd

A & H Davey's sister company Beech's Garage is surprisingly even older than 'Daveys'. Beech's began life in 1932 based in Massey Square, Burslem and its ERF truck distributorship began the following year. It is now the world's oldest ERF distributorship.

The firm was founded by Harry Beech and his son Norman. Harry Beech had worked for Vulcan trucks before moving from Southport to Burslem where he undertook general engineering work from a site in Church Lane.

The firm was very much a family concern and in addition to Harry's son his wife and daughters Madey, Anne and Mary were also actively involved in the early days.

Norman Beech was responsible for bringing the ERF franchise into his already impressive portfolio of agencies which then included MG, Rover, Guy.

It is to Norman Beech that the company owed its rise to prominence. During his lifetime Norman Beech built a national reputation for both service and personal integrity that is still a topic of conversation in the industry to this day.

After the second world war Norman bought surplus vehicles to strip for parts and rebuild them for civilian use. He stored vehicles at various locations including land at Bucknall where he was later to build his Leek New Road premises and at Procter's Yard in Bryant Street, Hanley.

In 1952 a garage at Leek New Road was built to store second hand vehicles and around that time Les Seddon, the firm's longest serving employee commenced his apprenticeship with Beechs; he still works as a valued member of the workshop team at Cliffe Vale. In 1960 an extension was added to the garage and the ERF operation was transferred from Hope Street, Hanley to Bucknall. The Hope Street site continued to operate as a garage for cars and light commercial vehicles until it closed in 1970.

Norman Beech died in 1969 leaving no children to follow him. The Edwards family, which ran an engineering company in Cobridge, took the company over in 1970. The Edwards presided over the slow demise of Beech's until, faced with liquidation, it was sold to its present owner, Barry Davey, in October 1983.

Above: *Unregistered 1948 ERF C15 in full livery.*
Below: *1948 ERF C15 12 tonner in service.*

Since 1983 by ongoing strategic management appointments the company has grown in stature and enhanced its reputation enormously. The company is now nationally recognised as a top performer within the ERF network and highly regarded throughout the transport industry.

The equipment used in the firm's formative years was all manually operated. In the workshops lifting tackle was mainly confined to ropes, block and tackle and pure muscle power. No ramps or vehicle lifts were used, although inspection pits were available - with no lights! Torches and improvised lighting were the order of the day. Oil for engines was always obtained in metal oil measures and poured into the engine, gearbox and rear axles - a tiresome and messy task. even drilling holes was a major operation often it was done with un-powered hand-drills - and the electric was quite often not available anyway. Many now-rare occurrences were common then. Les Seddon remembers the replacement of gearboxes and clutches out on the road at the scene of a breakdown. Often in the foulest weather, the only tools being spanners, the mechanic's strength, a small jack, a flask and a book of appropriate swear words! The passing down of this book through generations of mechanics becoming known as 'Passing the Buck'! Parts and accounting systems were then all controlled on a paperwork basis, a very long winded and time-consuming operation.

Today oil is controlled by computers, dispensed through air-driven delivery hoses and metered by computer. Lighting is of the best quality. Pits 65 ft in length now have high-illumination fire-proof lights and can accommodate the longest trucks and trailer combinations on the market. Parts levels and accounting systems are controlled by a computer system too. Lap top computers have even replaced the representative's notebook and pen.

Top: *Mr Arthur Davey being handed the log books by the General Manager of BRS. Onlooking is Mrs Hilda Davey and six of the new drivers.*
Above: *Beech's Garage premises in Leek Road, Hanley built in 1952 and their operating centre until the move in May 1995.*

the truck operator irrespective of the type or make of truck is a key element of the firm's success. The company propounded a unique after-sales principle for its industry; S.O.D. (Service on Demand) 'Yes is the answer.. now what's the question?'

Beech's supplier, ERF truck manufacturer of Sandbach in Cheshire, lead the field in providing electronic engine-management systems and, more recently, gas powered waste collection vehicles. Beech's has an enviable technical training programme that supports its 24 hour service levels. It is a recognised fact that in the event of a breakdown any truck on the road can quickly get the attention and support of a Beech's technician trained to deal with the highest levels of contemporary technology.

In Barry Davey's words 'we are what we repeatedly do; excellence can become a habit; this company is therefore committed to achieving excellence' sentiments which Harry Beech and Norman Beech would have recognised as being as true in 1933 as they are today.

Above: *A line-up of old and new lorries at the Beech's opening.* ***Below:*** *Barry and Ashley Davey outside the firm's premises.*

Truck defects can be diagnosed by a Global Positioning System (GPS) irrespective of the truck's location.

Truck whereabouts and movement can be traced in the same manner. Automatic transmission, controlled by computer, takes a high percentage of stress, pressure and responsibility from drivers.

It is sadly often overlooked fact that without the pioneers such as Norman Beech and his father venturing into the retail truck industry many of the so called giants of today would simply not exist.

Of the move to the present site from Bucknall in 1995 Barry Davey remembers establishing workshop equipment installations along with oil and grease stocks. 'All office layouts, computer cables and live real-time data that would be needed to be available from day one were secured prior to the move. New racking and storage equipment complete with locations for the tens of thousands of parts valued at over £500,000 were prepared to allow the firm to have them available immediately for their customers. New paperwork including letterheads, invoices, business cards and credit notes had to be printed; new telephones, new telephone systems, all communication data and customer information packages were all prepared in advance to ensure little or no disruption occurred to the level of service offered to customers. The prior planning and preparation for that major operation was so good that they moved lock, stock and barrel over a weekend and opened for business as usual on the Monday - a testimonial to the value of good planning and the worth of committed people'.
24 hour availability of a wide range of commercial and technical services for

At the shops

The young women in white dresses on their way into the department store are dressed in the height of 1949 fashion. They are both showing a pretty calf below the hemline length of the day. The utilitarian look of the earlier 1940s was swept away by the styles exploding out of the Parisian fashion houses. Out went the square cut military look. In came sloping shoulders, rounded bosoms, waspish waists and padded hips. Women looked and felt feminine once more. Men bothered little. The suit and homburg or trilby continued to be the uniform dress they wore around town. Women began to go to town hatless. That was unheard of in their mothers' day. Some hedged their bets and wore a headscarf. Tastes change. Before long, the 50s would come. Full skirts billowing out over net petticoats became the new rage. The attractive couple was off to check the latest additions to the range on sale at Bratt and Dyke. The building stood on the site of the old Roebuck Inn, Trinity Street. It was known as The Central when it was erected in 1896. Oliver Bratt and Henry Dyke had been in business together since 1876. When they opened their new store there was living accommodation provided for many of its shop assistants. They really could take their work home with them, for they never left the building. When the store closed in 1989, Hanley lost a classy old friend.

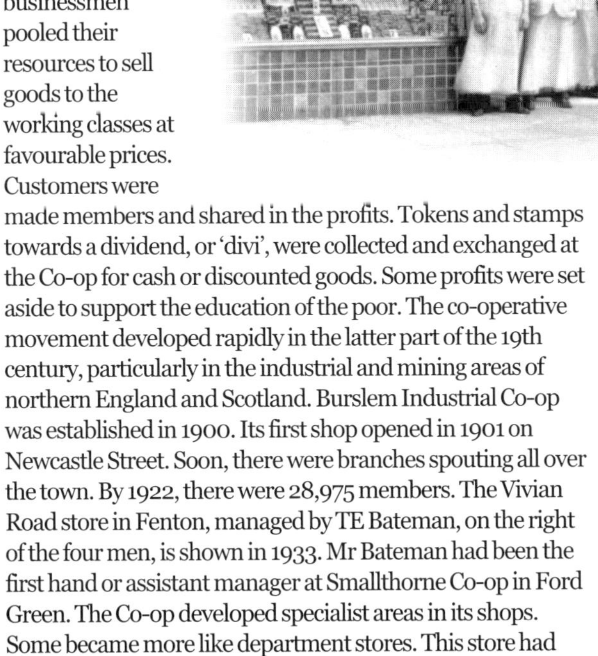

Right: In a little shop on Toad Lane, Rochdale a small acorn was planted. It grew into the Co-operative Society. In 1844, a group of businessmen pooled their resources to sell goods to the working classes at favourable prices. Customers were made members and shared in the profits. Tokens and stamps towards a dividend, or 'divi', were collected and exchanged at the Co-op for cash or discounted goods. Some profits were set aside to support the education of the poor. The co-operative movement developed rapidly in the latter part of the 19th century, particularly in the industrial and mining areas of northern England and Scotland. Burslem Industrial Co-op was established in 1900. Its first shop opened in 1901 on Newcastle Street. Soon, there were branches spouting all over the town. By 1922, there were 28,975 members. The Vivian Road store in Fenton, managed by TE Bateman, on the right of the four men, is shown in 1933. Mr Bateman had been the first hand or assistant manager at Smallthorne Co-op in Ford Green. The Co-op developed specialist areas in its shops. Some became more like department stores. This store had already separated part of its business into sections. Typical of attitudes was that the men took care of the meat counter. The women dealt with the gentler world of sweets and chocolates. All the employees had got ready for the photo call. Their clean, white overalls were stiffly starched for the occasion.

Below: What a paradise of footwear. Imelda Marcos, the wife of the powerful 1970s leader of the Philippines, would have had a field day window shopping. She was said to own 3,000 pairs of shoes. Mrs Marcos could have added to her collection from this impressive array. Since time immemorial, shoes have been made of leather. Kid leather, made from goatskin, has been used for women's dress shoes. Stepping out to a ball or on a visit to the opera, women need to look their best. Reptile leathers (alligator, lizard, and snake) have been popular, but animal rights activists have put an end to those. But, it is more than the material that is important. There is style and fashion to be considered. Wedge shapes, stiletto heels, pointed toes and platform soles come and go as tastes alter and fashion houses dictate. What is a girl to do? Sensible court shoes or slinky ankle straps? There is so much to be considered. In 17th-century Europe, boots were generally worn. In the 1960s we were back in them. Thigh high boots below a mini skirt and kinky boots, as worn by TV's 'Avengers' girls, were all the rage. During the rock and roll era, it had been high heeled stilettos that we tottered around on. They set off the swirling petticoated dresses of that age. Who wants to go out in trainers? Get down to the shoe shop for some class, but do not forget your credit card. Fashion does not come cheap.

In the 1950s the popularity of Hanley's Electricity House, on the corner of Piccadilly and Marsh Street, was a sign of the new affluence that had arrived. Labour saving devices were all the rage. We could afford them, just about. Unemployment was low and pay packets were full. Britain had turned the corner from those difficult postwar years. Housewives had struggled on Mondays, scrubbing collars, handwashing the laundry in large dolly tubs and squeezing the water out through the rollers of the mangle. Then it was fingers crossed and pray for a fine day as the washing was pegged on the line. Eventually, it was brought back in and the iron was heated up on the range and the laborious job of putting neat creases in everything began. Mum had to fit in sweeping the floor, whacking the dust from the carpet, polishing the tiles and donkey stoning the step. Even then, there was darning to be done and new clothes to be run up on the treadled sewing machine. Despite all that, she still had to prepare the evening meal and think what to put in dad's lunch box for the next day. Oh yes, we nearly forgot. The rearing of the kids was also her responsibility. No wonder she thanked God and the government for the better times. Automatic washing machines, tumble driers, electric irons, programmable cookers and fridges eased her burden. She still had it all to do for husbands rarely lifted a finger, but now she could grab five minutes to check out the hats in Raynes' millinery and gown shop.

Earning a crust

The Warrillow Collection

Conditions in the factories were poor. Dust in the potbanks led to pneumoconiosis, or 'potter's rot'. Workers suffered from lead poisoning, developing partial paralysis and problems with the nervous system. Tuberculosis and other infectious diseases were endemic. A health, report published in 1910, identified respiratory illness as the biggest cause of death. Factory conditions improved during the first half of the 20th century, but the potbanks still smoked on. At one stage there were 2,000 coal fired kilns pouring out their horrid fumes. In the 1950s successive Clean Air Acts cut back the amount of filth being released into the atmosphere. We could see the sky again.

Above: If ever there was a scene that demanded action, here you have it. Looking something like the aftermath of a nuclear holocaust, the Potteries landscape in the 1950s was about to change. Pictured near Hanley, the kiln chimneys and bottle ovens had been gushing out clouds of poisonous fumes for the better part of two centuries. We had become accustomed to wearing a blouse that was filthy with soot specks in a few short hours. When foggy November came, we were covered with smog. People walked around with little masks on their faces or hankies clutched to their mouths. This was the climate in which the children of the baby boom years were growing up. For days on end the sun was blotted out. As production exploded in the 19th century, so did the pollution. The Potteries became notorious for its low standards of health.

Top: 'Fresh air for the Potteries' was the ironic title of this postcard. It was the sort of scene that Ernest Warrillow, the social historian, used in his lantern slide lectures. It illustrates quite graphically the conditions in which people existed in 1910. Old timers tell of going to work more by feel and memory than by using their sight. William Blake took the photograph. He was a stationer who took up the new hobby of photography late in the 19th century. Although his most productive period was in the first quarter of the 20th century, he carried on his work into the 1940s. A firm member of the temperance movement, Blake was something of a social firebrand. He used his images to show the devil that was capi-talism and how it damaged the lives of ordinary folk. That message was clear in this postcard. A collection of his work was purchased by the City Museum with the help of a grant from the National Lottery.

The Warrillow Collection

Above: This potter is working inside one of the kilns at Longton that was still in operation in 1950. He is carefully balancing two saggars on his head as he shows off his skill for the camera. Saggar is one of the few special pottery terms of which most people from outside the Potteries have heard. They may not know what they are, but the older public remembers where it first heard the word. In the 1950s and 1960s there was a very popular panel game called 'What's My Line'. A version of it was revived in the late 1980s. A group of personalities had to guess the occupations of different individuals chosen from across the board. Many had straightforward jobs, but the best entertainment was to be had from those who had unusual jobs. Guests had to sign in, mime their job and then answer 'yes' or 'no' to the questions posed to them by the panel. Usually the 'experts' won. But, on one memorable occasion, they were completely stumped. The contestant that famous day worked as a saggar maker's bottom knocker! Saggars are the clay containers in which flat wares were packed to prevent warping and pot figures placed to prevent sagging. Hence the name. The saggars were then placed in the ovens for the firing process to begin. The bottom knocker's main job was to beat out the fire-clay for making the saggar bottoms. No wonder the panel lost that day!

Below centre: In a kind of through the keyhole picture of the inside of a bottle oven, there is just enough room for the onlooker to appreciate the size of the kiln. Row upon row of saggars has been piled high as even more are being added. Each saggar contained any number of plates, dishes and figurines. The potters packed them into the baked clay containers so that they would not become deformed under the high temperatures. Fired at high temperature, the kilns were fuelled by coal. The process of stacking the saggars was called 'settling in'. The trick of balancing them on his head was not just done for the camera. This was the age old way of moving the saggars about. It is not that remarkable a feat. We have all seen newsreels of African and Asian women carrying large water pots or bundles of possessions great distances on their heads. Anything that a native of Eritrea or the Punjab can do, so could a Potteries' man. It kept his hands free to climb the ladder and put the next saggar in place. There were quite a few rungs to climb before he reached the top of each stack. Hundreds of containers, filled with thousands of items, would be baked in a single firing. The ovens would be cleared and the whole process begun again.

Taking the biscuit

To anyone else other than someone from the Potteries, the word 'biscuits' conjures up thoughts of digestives, gipsy creams and rich teas. Not so, if you are from this part of the world. To us the word means the first firing given to porcelain and earthenware before it has been glazed. The pottery industry has its own peculiar vocabulary. Saggars, wedging, bat printing, sprigging, jollies and jiggers are all words that confuse the outsider. Every good potter knows them all, and many more that relate to his craft.

In medieval times and through to the days of the Tudors, the pottery industry was a simple one. In the small rural communities that eventually grew to become the Potteries, it was a small scale enterprise. Potters worked individually or in families from home. They used the clay they found near their homes and supplied local markets with their crude wares. As the 17th century dawned, the craftsmen were in competition with those in the larger towns and cities, as well as ones from abroad. The use of coal as a fuel helped the Staffordshire potters compete as many rivals were still using wood as their fuel. Soon, the local industry was carving an important niche for itself across the Midlands as the fame and expertise of Burslem pottery, in particular, spread.

Burslem calls itself the 'mother town of the Potteries'. By the early 1600s it had built itself a formidable reputation for making earthenware. Its butter pots were especially well known and led to it being known as Butter Pot Town. But it was the middle of the 18th century that saw the ceramics industry make giant strides forward. Josiah Wedgwood, a son of Burslem, worked in his father's pottery business. A skilful hand at the potter's wheel, he contracted smallpox and this disease laid him low for a long time. This gave him the chance to research and experiment. He went into partnership with Thomas Whieldon and produced his famous green glaze. Wedgwood then went it alone, producing cream coloured ware that was popularised by Queen Charlotte, wife of George III. He built the Etruria factory in the early 1770s, making his renowned ornamental vases and jasperware. In 1793 Thomas Minton founded a factory in Stoke upon Trent. He is best remembered for his Willow pattern, but also produced cream and blue printed earthenware majolica. In the 1820s he manufactured bone china and became the best known source of dinnerware for the middle and upper classes. Around 1800 Josiah Spode introduced his brand of porcelain, producing elaborate services and outsize vases, lavishly decorated and gilded in the Empire style. His early work was often influenced by Japanese patterns.

These three men were amongst the greatest influences on the ceramics industry in the Potteries. Throughout Victorian times potbanks and their yards seemed to cover great areas of the Potteries. Bottle shaped ovens dominated the skyline. These kilns belched out smoke and filth across the district, but were seen as a necessary evil in the economy of the Potteries. Later, they were enclosed in buildings, so that only the top part of the chimney could be seen. In those days the potbank yards were disorganised, cramped and messy affairs. These contrasted with the more ornate architecture of the new factories and buildings that grew around them. Enoch Wood's Burslem works even had a gateway with castle style battlements!

The dictionary describes ceramics as being the manufacture of any product made essentially from a non metallic mineral. Such a simplistic definition really does take the biscuit.

Bottom: Making sanitary ware was perhaps too rude a job for women. Whatever the reason, this was a men only work room. A mixture of toilet bowls, chamber pots, cisterns and bedpans was being turned out. Tourists to the museums and factory shops that put on tours often ignore this part of the pottery business. For many, pottery is a world of crockery, attractive vases and figures from legend. They are often the gloss on the substance. Tiles and sanitary ware have been them mainstay of many a business that never threw a single pot or figurine on the potter's wheel. As housing conditions improved and better sanitation was provided by the town councils, firms such as Twyford and Armitage prospered and profited. From late Victorian times and onwards, these and other firms combined engineering and ceramic skills to good effect. Baths and wash basins replaced the old tin contraption in front of the fire. As indoor lavatories took over from outside privvies, lifestyles changed. So did the emphasis of the ceramics industry. Further adaptations were made. In the 20th century, ceramic insulation for the electricity industry created a new market. At the same time, factory conditions gradually improved. From 1899 all workshops had to have a ventilation system fitted. Workshops had to be cleaned daily. The amount of lead in glazes was drastically reduced. However, it was not until 1949 that there was a full restriction imposed on glazes that did not have a low solubility of lead.

Right: CW Brown (1882-1961) got all Potteries' life into one scene in this piece of artwork. All that was important to the region is crammed into this one memorable panorama. Twyford's Works has produced sanitary ware for generations and has been a major employer well known across the country. Every single reader will have seen the name emblazoned on toilet bowls in houses, hotels and public conveniences from John o' Groats to Land's End. Behind the factory gates is Brown's commentary on life as we knew it in 1937. The bottle ovens blasted forth their ghastly smoke, but provided the economy that gave us three square meals a day. Elsewhere, the factory chimneys, collieries and iron and steel works do much the same. Even the railway has its steam locomotive playing the same dual role. It helped bring both prosperity and pollution to the Potteries. The ugly gasholders show their unattractive face in front of the real message of Brown's painting. Behind everything is the parish church. Its graveyard is waiting for all of us. Many arrived there too soon, killed by the pollution before they could enjoy the prosperity. CW Brown was a local artist who painted brightly coloured scenes in a naive style. His work had some similarities with Lancashire artist, LS Lowry. But Brown had a keener and more perceptive eye for working conditions. He had worked in the coalfields and drew on that experience. After his retirement in 1948, he devoted even more time to painting industry, people and the local environment.

This was one of the scores of smaller potteries scattered haphazardly across Stoke-on-Trent. These glost and biscuit kilns were at Barlow Street and Uttoxeter Road in Longton. Glost firing took place after the glazing process. The saggars that had been filled for the first biscuit firing were restacked and sealed to keep out the sulphur fumes that might discolour the newly glazed pottery. The ovens would burn for over 24 hours before it was time to remove the saggars once more. It was normal to have different kilns for the biscuit and glost firing. The glost wares were taken carefully from the ovens and checked for imperfections. They were gently banged against each other. A clear ringing sound meant that the pottery was of good quality. Longton, sometimes known to locals as 'Neck End', was a place of ironworks and coal mines during the 18th century. As the 19th century began, it had begun to turn into one of the main centres for producing bone china. Bottle ovens popped up all over the place. Shops, homes and drinking houses appeared in their midst. There seemed no real system or plan as businesses and houses appeared in a higgledy piggledy fashion. Not surprisingly, the environment was amongst the worst in the area. Life expectancy was low. The harsh conditions continued into the 20th century. It was only after World War II that the bulldozers moved in and cleared the worst away. Heinz soup was about all that did give a glow.

The Old Foley Pottery - pottery for posterity

Pottery is one of the longest lasting materials made by mankind. Archaeologists working on historic sites throughout the world turn up ceramic pieces which are not merely hundreds but thousands of years old. With that in mind one may care to pause for a moment to reflect that pottery produced today in Stoke will, in all likelihood, one day be examined, identified and categorised by our far distant descendants perhaps millennia from now. And those future archaeologists will undoubtedly be impressed by what they find.

Stoke-on-Trent is a mixture of towns including Longton, Cobridge and Burslem, names which are often unfamiliar to those from other parts of Britain - unless that is they own a piece of pottery fired in one of the bottle kilns which once littered the city. Today almost all of those kilns have disappeared and many of the existing pottery buildings are crumbling whilst others have not survived the arrival of massive foreign competition. Even so, despite all that change, destruction and retrenchment, new life has emerged.

The Hadida group began looking in the Stoke area for a supplier in the late 1970s to produce a range of ceramics for its expanding bathroom business. By 1984 rather than importing the shapes from Japan, to maintain the market they had created Hadida decided that it should manufacture in the

Below: *Rose Water Sprinkler - Charles Bourne (1820).*
Bottom: *An early plate transfer reputed to show the Old Foley Pottery.*

UK and so bought a small factory in Bute Street, Fenton which they equipped with completely new machinery as well as investing in a considerable number of moulds.

By the beginning of 1989 however Hadida Fine Bone China Ltd of Fenton had outgrown its premises and, right on cue, James Kent Ltd at the Old Foley Pottery in King Street, Fenton came up for sale. Hadida's owners had admired James Kent's shapes and designs for some time so buying the firm was not a difficult decision to make.

It was in 1967 that the Hadida group began life in London when Michael Hadida started up a business importing shower curtains. Despite the inevitable initial problems associated with starting a new business - including the never to be forgotten three day week in 1974 - the new firm expanded into bathroom accessories. The firm was soon selling to department stores in the UK such as John Lewis and House of Fraser and eventually grew to build up export markets in France, Germany and the USA.

The James Kent company was founded at the Old Foley Pottery in Longton in 1897 and is located on the old turnpike road between Fenton and the present Longton. It is reputed that pottery has been made on the site since 1689 although no hard evidence of this early production has yet come to light.

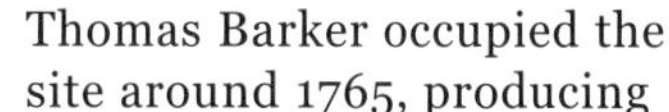

Thomas Barker occupied the site around 1765, producing mainly red stonewares, white salt-glazed stonewares and creamwares. His daughter Elizabeth married Josiah Spode II in 1775 and following her death in 1782 ownership of the works passed to the Spode family. Samuel Spode ran the works until his retirement in 1812 when Charles Bourne, a partner at the nearby Fenton Park Colliery and an established earthenware manufacturer, saw his chance to expand into porcelain manufacture with the purchase of the Foley pottery. In the early days he produced large quantities of earthenwares and stonewares as well as the manufacture of porcelain.

Top left: *A Chrysanthemum Jug, circa 1820 - pattern number 19 - together with the original mould recently found at "The Foley Pottery".* ***Top right:*** *A rare Charles Bourne perfume bottle, circa 1820.* ***Above left:*** *Chrysanthemum Jug, pattern number 5, circa 1820.* ***Below:*** *A Charles Bourne dessert plate circa 1825.*

The early porcelains were all teawares for the lower end of the market but by 1815 a teaware pattern book was started and although the early designs were simple they progressed into elaborate patterns to rival those produced by Spode and Ridgeway. Production soon increased to include fine dessert and ornamental wares whose quality equalled the best made in Staffordshire Potteries at this time.

Charles Bourne was quick to take advantage of market opportunities. In 1816 one of the principal makers of stoneware jugs was David Wilson, but he died in the June of that year and his brother was unsuccessful in continuing the business and was made bankrupt in July 1817. This left a gap in the market which Charles Bourne took full advantage of and began the production of a range of stonewares which he marked with a Chrysanthemum pad on the base.

By 1828 Charles Bourne was in declining health and resigned his partnership in the Fenton Park Colliery partnership and offered the factory "for sale or let". In 1832 the works was let to John Mayer who continued production much as in Charles Bourne's time making it difficult to distinguish items made by John Mayer Charles Bourne.

John Mayer didn't enjoy much luck at the Foley and in 1837 a glost kiln needed to be rebuilt following damage caused by mine workings and in

Below: *The whole company at Westminster in 1947. Ruth Kent is at the front centre.* ***Left:*** *A 1950s advertisement for 'Old Foley' ware produced by James Kent.*

December 1840 his business ceased and his stock and furniture was subsequently sold by sheriff's auction. By 1842 the Bourne family had sold the works and it was then occupied by John Hawley, but he could not sustain such a large works and in 1853 part of the site was sold off and operations continued on a smaller scale. In 1872 the works was taken over by Moore & Co and for the first time became known as "The Old Foley Pottery". Finally, James Kent purchased the works in 1897 and the present day business was built up from there becoming James Kent Ltd in 1913. The words 'Old Foley' or 'Ye Old Foley' sometimes being added to the Kent Trademark from the earliest times.

Salad Days

Presenting a selection from "Salad Days"

In buying the Foley works James Kent 'inherited' a wonderful collection of Victorian moulds for producing jugs, vases and other pieces from that era. In addition a considerable number of hand engraved copper rollers were unearthed which had been produced more than a hundred years earlier and which depicted rural scenes of the Regency period. These enabled the company to build a substantial range of giftware and achieve Royal recognition in the coronation year of 1911 when it was requested to produce blue and white ware for King George V and Queen Mary.

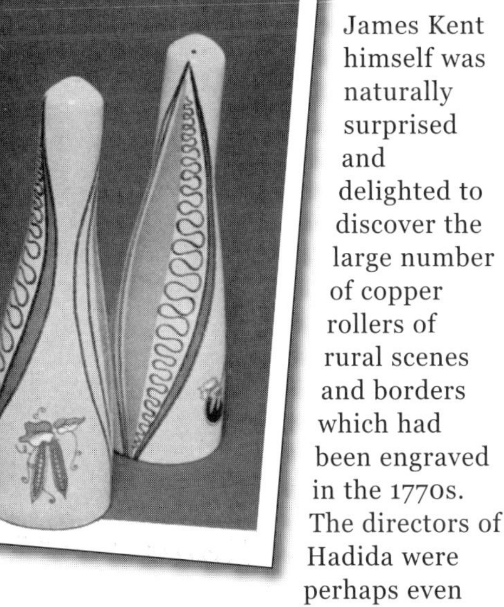

James Kent himself was naturally surprised and delighted to discover the large number of copper rollers of rural scenes and borders which had been engraved in the 1770s. The directors of Hadida were perhaps even more surprised and delighted in finding that they were still there in the archives!

The first half of the twentieth century saw James Kent become a major force in the ceramic field, mostly giftware, and particularly in exports where some 80 per cent of its production went, especially the Australian market. Between the wars a vast range of table and giftware was produced including delicate floral chintz prints, moulded and embossed vases and jugs and stylised landscape patterns characterised by tall trees and quaint cottages reminiscent of the work of Clarice Cliff. The 'Old Foley' or 'Ye Old Foley' marks were retained after the second world war despite the move to premises in Fountain Street, Fenton.

From the outset James Kent was mainly a producer of good-class medium-priced earthenware for household use but he also made richly decorated table services and fancies. The pottery however earned its reputation as specialist in chintz and floral patterns, produced from the 1920s onwards. Even in the 1960s the firm was heavily promoting its Rosalynde chintz pattern dinner, tea and table fancies portraying the English moss rose.

Above: *The 1960s contemporary modern range of 'Salad Days' fancies.*

Occasionally the firm produced children's ware such as a nursery set designed by Peter Fraser in the 1940s. The firm also made some more contemporary lines in the 1920s and 1930s and even in the 1960s produced a contemporary modern range of tableware fancies in shades of red, yellow and green which it called Salad Days, although production of those was short-lived. In the 1950s the pottery produced a wide range of traditional Staffordshire figures, animal groups and Toby jugs.

At its height more than three hundred worked at the James Kent pottery; hard times lay ahead however. In the 1950s on the death of the founder his son Philip Kent took over running the business followed, in turn after his death in 1960, by Miss Ruth Kent.

James Kent's daughter Ruth ran the business throughout the sixties and seventies travelling all over the world selling the James Kent name.

In many respects it was Ruth Kent who had been a mainstay of the business for many years. However she was no ordinary woman. Her modern approach to business saw her leading trade missions to America at a time when such a feat for a woman was truly ground-breaking.

By the 1970s with increasing competitive pressures world wide the company lost direction. James Kent Ltd was forced down market and struggled to maintain its high standards. When Ruth Kent retired in the early 1980s the company was first acquired by Bayer chemicals and subsequently three other owners before Hadida came along in 1989.

Kents was bought by Bayer (UK)Ltd in 1981 and by Fleshpots (UK) Ltd in 1986.

The 'Fleshpots' company had been formed in 1978 and soon acquired a reputation for unusual modern ceramics such as a three piece stack of casseroles in the shape of a human form or its 'Hollywood' range - life sized portrait busts of celebrities such as Marilyn Monroe, Charlie Chaplin, Elvis Presley and Clark Gable. The moulds remain in the company archives. According to Clare Hadida the three piece casserole set in the shape of a woman's body is one of her odder discoveries. 'The first piece is the woman's bottom, the second her belly button and the third her bust. I think it's probably the strangest thing we've found to date'.

Due to an expanding order book Fleshpots, very much smaller than James Kent Ltd but in need of extra manufacturing capacity, acquired James Kent on 15th March 1986. Fleshpots had expected Kent products to be a handicap but it soon became clear that on the continent and in the USA James Kent had a very good image and, as others would discover, a mould store containing a multitude of original plaster moulds from all the major stylistic periods including Art Nouveau and Art Deco teapots and cups and saucers, 1940s utility ware and 1950s contemporary ware.

A new marketing strategy was arrived at with four brand names:

***Top:** A limited edition jug issued to commemorate 100 years of James Kent in 1997. **Above right:** Lydia - part of the Du Barry collection. The Du Barry chintz range was named after a play in London which Ruth's brother had seen. **Right:** A Du Barry tea pot and cruet set.*

the 'James Kent' brand would produce traditional fine earthenware and concentrated on contract work for major stores; 'Fleshpots' would be the label of modern innovative pieces of often risky ceramics maintaining a contemporary presence; 'Old Foley' would be the label of rejuvenated classics - not copies or fake antiques but genuine models cast from original moulds and decorated according to the period. The fourth and final brand label in this period was 'Foley' - craft orientated ceramics. This latter label comprised the limited edition Next Collection and featured such artists as Gail Fox, Carol McNicoll, Janice Tchalenko, Hinchcliff and Barber, Karen Bunting, Sabina Teuteberg, Jane Wilingale and Joanne and Andrew Young.

The Fleshpots interlude however was to last only a single year; James Kent Ltd being bought by Rock, an engineering suppliers in 1987 - and later that same year by a holding company County Potteries Ltd. The holding company changed its name to Carlton and Kent in 1989 and went into receivership almost immediately thereafter before being acquired by M R Hadida Ltd and renamed James Kent (1989) Ltd.

Hadida spent nine years and a considerable sum of money in bringing the factory and offices up to the standard its directors felt appropriate to run an efficient operation. For example ware is no longer carried up and down staircases where previously it had been - sometimes twice during production. Hadida is now turning its attention to the historical legacy of the James Kent business: the Kent name was known world wide in the 1930s for its chintz designs. Clare Hadida is now reproducing some of those exclusive designs and marketing them through the company website. The intention is to evolve products of the very highest quality using some of the hundreds of shapes available in the James Kent archives. The first two designs which went into production were 'Du Barry' and 'Hydrangea'. Some of the original Du Barry pieces have incidentally fetched substantial prices at a sale at Christies in London in recent times.

The Hydrangea and Du Barry tea services were not issued until the lithographing techniques had been perfected. Trimming the chintz patterns around the handles and ensuring that joins do not show is not an easy task.

The items now being made at James Kent will be going to collectors all over the world. The expectations of quality are very high and Hadida intend that its customers will not be disappointed. The quality is now in fact superior to that of the originals. In addition to the two new designs already mentioned, another three designs Lydia, Rosalynde and Ruth Kent have been added. The company has also begun to make use of the vast number of copper rollers in the archives to produce Rosarie and 18th Century Chintz.

After facing a somewhat uncertain future in the 1980s, James Kent is now safely under the Hadida umbrella and going from strength to strength. And who knows perhaps our long distant descendants will not merely be picking broken pot shards from the ruins of our present civilisation but will even be going along to the shops and still be able to buy their new dinner services from Hadida's current James Kent range! WWW.hadida.co.uk.

Top: *'Ruth Kent', the service being named after the founder's daughter who steered the company in the mid 1900s.* ***Above left:*** *The Rosarie coffee pot and the 18th Century tea pot.* ***Right:*** *The company's latest range - 'Manhattan Lime'.* ***Below:*** *Foley - Janice Tchalenko Second Range.*

Ceramics with style and sophistication

If you lack class then, when you hear Rossini's rousing William Tell Overture, all you can think of is the Lone Ranger galloping off into the sunset. The same may be true of those who can only link Portmeirion with the cult TV show, 'The Prisoner'. The vision of Patrick McGoohan being chased by a large balloon lingers in the minds of those who have never visited the fabulous and mildly eccentric village where the series was filmed. Portmeirion is situated in North Wales and was the brainchild of sir Clough Williams-Ellis. Fascinated by Latin design and architecture, Sir Clough built his own replica Italian style village. It soon became the place to visit for those coming to North Wales to see something both different and unique. Sir Clough could often be seen strolling in his beloved creation, resplendent in his plus twos and colourful waistcoat. Today it still attracts thousands of visitors and is often used by companies as a conference centre or group holiday base. The great man's daughter inherited her father's love of style and sophistication. Susan Williams-Ellis studied art under the tutelage of the world renowned Henry Moore and Graham Sutherland in the 1930s. She and husband Euan Cooper-Willis ran the Portmeirion shop in the years after World War II. She combined this job with designing pottery for the shop to sell. Not surprisingly, with her background, by the 1960s she had achieved such success that she was able to acquire two small potteries in Stoke-on-Trent. She was so innovative in her approach that people in the world of art, design and especially ceramics soon took note of this rising star. With her background, to call her company Portmeirion Potteries was the obvious choice.

It was in 1972 that the major breakthrough came. Susan launched 'The Botanic Garden', a range of tableware that was a best-seller all across the globe. Aided by her gift for originality, linked to good, modern design, Portmeirion products quickly rose from the backwaters to be a force to be reckoned with in the ceramic world.

Above: *One of the first designs featuring a lady in a Welsh costume.* ***Below:*** *The pretty town of Portmeirion from where the pottery originated.*

As well as the three retail outlets in Stoke-on-Trent, London's Kensington Church Street boasts a showroom and shop. But, the success story has spread even further. Inroads have been made across 'the big pond'. Portmeirion has a showroom on Madison Avenue, New York and another subsidiary company in Canada, with a large showroom in Toronto. By the beginning of the 21st century there were distributors and agents in more than 50 countries.

Portmeirion Potteries, with such attractive collections as its 'Dawn and Dusk' range, is often a must on a bride's gift list. However, if she asks for the 'Prisoner Number Six' collection, then that girl lacks style.

Above left: *Susan Williams Ellis working on one of her designs.* ***Below:*** *Botanic Garden, launched in 1972, the design that put Portmeirion Potteries on the map.*

In the present day its impact is only seriously rivalled by the likes of Wedgwood, Denby and Royal Doulton. Portmeirion's ability in developing excellent marketing skills to match the quality of its products will see it expand its market sector through the future development of non ceramic items. These will include placemats, trays, candles and glassware that will enhance the Portmeirion ceramic designs. Much of that expansion will be in the hands of the next generation of this gifted family. Susan's daughters, Anwyl Cooper-Willis and Angharad Menna, have inherited the Williams-Ellis artistic skills and are actively concerned with the development of Portmeirion tableware, crockery, kitchenware and giftware. 'The Botanic Garden' has been the source of continued review and modification in the 30 years since its launch. In 1982 'Pomona' was unveiled. Its fruit pattern was an immediate hit and provided Portmeirion with another big winner. The festive 'Holly and the Ivy', which appeared in 1996, was a further example of popular creativity. The contemporary 'Seasons' collection was launched in 1999 using Susan's mandarin shape, with Anwyl co-ordinating the collection.

Although the company's base is in Stoke, success has seen it spread its wings far beyond the head office. There is the factory at Longton and the distribution centre in Fenton.

Two centuries of great British pottery

Churchill China is an amalgamation of a number of family owned potteries. Owned today by the Roper family, the company history can be traced back to the Bridgwood family which began trading in 1795. Today it is a plc with a multi-million pound turnover, employing some 1,400 people in its four factories. It is split into two divisions, known as Dining In and, hardly surprisingly, Dining Out. The former looks after the retail side of the business and the latter the hospitality, or catering market. Both divisions operate on a worldwide basis, selling dinnerware and associated tabletop products to retailers such as department stores, supermarkets and to hoteliers and restauranteurs. The Dining In division received the Queen's Award for export achievement in both 1988 and 1993.

The Dining Out division was awarded ISO accreditation in 1994. Its success has been put down to reliability in meeting orders and the quality of its customer service products. The control of the group is still in the hands of the Roper family, though by being floated on the Stock Exchange in 1994 Churchill China now has a wide and diverse range of investors.

It was in the days when The American War of Independence and the French Revolution were recent memories that Samuel Bridgwood joined forces with his brother-in-law Richard Johnson. They made Staffordshire earthenware at the Anchor Works, Longton that now forms part of the Dining Out factory. The partnership was not longlived. The two men went their separate ways. Samuel died in 1805 and it was his widow, Kitty, who kept the pottery going. In 1814 she bought the factory that Richard Johnson owned to add to her own premises. Her son, Sampson, was brought into the firm around this time as manager of one of the factories. The times were changing. Earthenware pottery was gradually being replaced by bone china, although its popularity was slow in coming. However, by 1852 Bridgwood's was employing 150 people to work its three oven factory.

The following year his son, Samuel, was officially taken on when the company became called Sampson Bridgwood and Son As well as being an important employer in the area, Sampson Bridgwood was considered a big enough personality to become the first Chief Bailiff of Longton. Both he and his son were to become magistrates.

SAMPSON BRIDGWOOD & SON
ANCHOR POTTERY, LONGTON, STAFFORDSHIRE.
TEA, BREAKFAST, and DESSERT SERVICES, TRINKET and DEJEUNER SETS, PLAQUES, VASES, &c., in China of the FINEST Quality.
DINNER, TEA, and TOILET SERVICES, JUGS, PLAQUES, &c., IN Porcelaine Opaque, OR FINE White Granite.
Plain and Slightly Decorated Goods; also New Shapes and Decorations of the most Artistic Character.
EXPORT ORDERS, FOR LARGE OR SMALL QUANTITIES, PROMPTLY EXECUTED.
LONDON SHOW ROOMS:—15, CHARTERHOUSE St., HOLBORN CIRCUS. Mr. J. W. PULLEY, Agent.

Top left: *Edward Roper, Managing Director of Broadhursts 1922-1929 and chairman from 1930-1941.* ***Above:*** *An advertisement for the firm in the days of Sampson Bridgwood and Son.* ***Below:*** *The main entrance circa 1890.* ***Left:*** *An 1880s advertisement.*

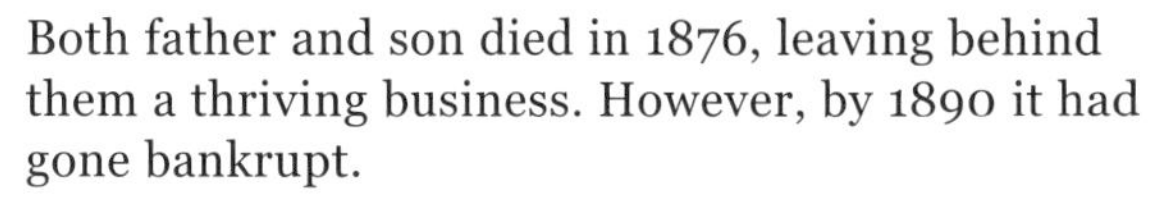

Both father and son died in 1876, leaving behind them a thriving business. However, by 1890 it had gone bankrupt.

As the Bridgwoods were achieving distinction as potters, in 1847 Peter Hampson, James Broadhurst and nephew William Broadhurst set up a partnership at the Green Dock Works, Longton. By 1854 James Broadhurst was going it alone. Within two years he had involved his son in the company. They made both china and earthenware. When James died in 1858 his widow, Drusilla, continued the family concern at the Crown Works. After her death, three years later, it was James Broadhurst II who assumed the major role in running what had become called James Broadhurst and Sons. He had a flair for the trade and was also possessed of good sense. He started registering his own designs. These included an Oriental scene for decorating jugs, an intertwined garland plate border and a flag and crest of the Empire of Brazil. James was also concerned with more than making a profit. He busied himself in getting better working conditions for children that helped cut down their hours, gave more work to women and encouraged children to go to school. His obituary in 1897 said that he was 'one of the pioneers of the newer style of manufacture'.

The Churchill China company's modern history probably goes back to 1922 when Edward Roper bought a half share in Broadhust's pottery. He was joined by son Peter in 1928. During World War II the factory was closed down. Edward did not survive the war, so, after seeing active service in the RAF, Peter reopened the firm and embarked on a sweeping modernisation programme. By 1960 Peter had been

joined by his son Stephen. Five years further on the Ropers bought Bridgwoods. It had been bought up and run by the Aynsley family since 1890. Stephen Roper's brother, Andrew, joined the firm in 1973. Myott Meakin and Crownford China were taken over in the early 1990s when the group became known as Churchill China plc.

In line with Churchill's strategy of building it's business at the higher end of the market, in the early 1990s the group purchased the exclusive rights, brands and intellectual property of Queen's Fine Bone China. This has taken the group into the bone china market. Since then, the group has invested more in supplying bone china products, notably in the acquisition of Wren in 1998. More recently the Churchill group has purchased the intellectual property, stock and goodwill of James Sadler, a manufacturer of collectable teapots. By continuing to invest in strengthening its product portfolio and utilising its factories, it will ensure the safety of existing jobs and the name of Churchill will continue to be an important one in both the hospitality and retail markets worldwide.

Top left: *Making transfers for the ceramics.* ***Above right:*** *The new RHS endorsed Applebee collection.* ***Below:*** *Staff celebrating the Queen's Award for export achievement in 1993.*

On the roofs and floors of the World

Since the first hard baked brick appeared in Mesopotamia some 5,000 years ago clay has sheltered more people, and covered their floors more effectively than any other natural material. Yet how many of us spare the time to glance up at the roofs which adorn our towns and cities, or look beneath our feet in many homes and public buildings to admire the skill of the manufacturers who have produced the wonderful tiles which shelter us from the elements and adorn our buildings and their floors?

For more than 175 years the craftsmen of Daniel Platt at the Brownhills Tileries at Tunstall have been turning the richest Etruria marl into the finest natural clay tiles of unsurpassed beauty for use on floors and roofs.

Daniel Platt have been creating fine quality clay tiles since 1822, and yet the company's history can be traced back even further. For when in 1978 Daniel Platt acquired the established and respected family business of Wheatly and Co of Springfield Tileries Newcastle under Lyme it also gained a history which stretches back to before 1819.

The factory occupied by Daniel Platt at Brownhills was established by two brothers Howard and Richard Haywood on twenty acres of land bought from John Wedgwood and John Wood. The factory was first listed in the Potteries' Trade directory in 1822 as a brick tile and quarry manufacturers and pipe works.

A survey of 1848 indicates that in those days the site comprised a brick and tile factory, a canal basin and warehouses, six cottages and Brownhills Villa. The factory occupied some thirteen of the site's twenty acres.

The Haywoods must have been doing well for themselves and by 1854 had acquired a London depot in Paddington.

Brownhills Villa was the Haywood brothers' home and was described as an elegant house on four acres of land.

The Haywoods retired in the late 1850s, leasing the factory to the virtually unknown Garret brothers, though retaining the rest of the site for themselves.

Below: *Making quarry tiles circa 1940s/50s.*

In 1867 the Garret brothers were succeeded by the partnership of Boulton, Burnett and Platt. (The 'Platt' member of the partnership being one John Platt, the father of Daniel Platt) Census data from the period indicates that the firm was then employing fifty hands, probably a similar number to those which had been employed for the previous thirty years.

Ownership of the factory passed from the Haywood brothers to William Shoobridge in 1874 following the death of the Haywood brothers. George Boulton their tenant died in 1886 and the factory appears to have stood empty for ten years until it was taken over by Daniel Platt in 1896.

Daniel Platt was born in Madeley in 1843 the son of John Platt a coal miner and the one time partner of George Boulton. Daniel worked as a grocer and cheese factor and later, following a highly advantageous marriage, holding a farm of 119 acres where he employed thirty-five workers.

In the final decades of the 19th century Daniel Platt followed his own father's career and became involved in tile manufacture with a factory at Harpfield and a company called the Harpfield Tile Company. Eventually Daniel acquired the lease of the factory at Brownhills, following which the company changed its name to Daniel Platt and Son Ltd

Five of Daniel Platt's own six sons eventually joined him in the business. In 1896 the Platts spent £5,000 on new ovens and machinery whilst William Shoobridge spent £1,000 restoring the dilapidated premises. In fact between 1895 and 1900 the Platt family spent more than £10,000 improving the factory. By 1912 most of the older buildings on the site had been demolished and others rebuilt including 14 new ovens. The five of Daniel's sons working in the business became partners in 1902 following his death in 1901. Business was mainly concentrated at the Brownhills factory by the end of World War I.

Although the firm also used a factory in Stoke Old Road, now used by the Diamond Refractories, since the second world war production has been confined to the factory at Brownhills, Tunstall.

Today Platt's reputation for high quality floor and roof tiles with a variety of fittings manufactured from Staffordshire clay - the worlds finest - ensure that the firm's products are in high demand by builders, contractors, architects and discerning private householders across the length and breadth of Britain.

Above left: *An exhibition stand showing the whole range of tiles produced by the firm before the second world war.* ***Above right:*** *Emptying tiles out of the Beehive Kilns.*

Falcon Pottery - still flying high

How many readers we wonder can glance at their mantlepiece and see an exquisite example of Victorian earthenware resting there, or perhaps a 1960s Dalek plate or novelty animal, all made at Hanley's Falcon Pottery?

The story of J H Weatherby & Sons Ltd of Falcon Pottery began in 1891 when the firm's founder the 48 year old John Henry Weatherby set up his own business at Pinnox Street in Tunstall.

An orphan, although with potters in his family for at least 150 years, J H Weatherby had earlier worked as a thrower and turner at William Wood's pottery. On leaving Wood's John Henry first became a partner in Whittaker Edge & Co at the Hallfield Pottery in Hanley, very near to Falcon Pottery, before setting up on his own account in Tunstall.

The new firm initially concentrated on manufacturing general earthenware: dinnerware and teaware, ewers and basins - and those now forgotten articles, cuspidors.

At the outset several family members helped the new business including John Weatherby's aunts. Eventually both John Weatherby's sons Samuel Mawdesley Weatherby and John Henry Weatherby junior were to join the family business - although initially not as partners.

The firm had to leave Tunstall in 1892 due to the higher wage rates there compared to Hanley. John Weatherby had to pay compensation to get out of the lease and moved to Hanley almost broke. The cost of the move took most of the available capital so he sold all the wares he could from Tunstall and transported the remaining equipment on wagons to Hanley, the family loading the wagons themselves to save money. All the family, aunts included, rallied round to work for nothing to allow the firm to continue. Nor was everything smooth running at the new premises: Falcon Pottery had been unused for some time and the bottle ovens were so damp they required three firings before a satisfactory piece of biscuitware could be glazed.

Falcon Pottery was incidentally originally in High Street before that road was renamed Town Road and, finally, Old Town Road.

Falcon Pottery was formed from several other factories previously on the site such as the Gelson Works and the Cobden works; records of them can be traced back as far as 1779.

In 1892 when John Weatherby and his family arrived in Hanley, pottery was all hand made, hand thrown and turned - a far cry from today's automatic and semi automatic machines. Undoubtedly the work was far harder and time consuming than it is today although no doubt the sense of satisfaction to be gained from producing a craftsman made article was high.

Above left: *The company founder and his sons from left to right Mr SM Weatherby, Mr JH Weatherby Snr, and Mr JH Weatherby Jr.*
Below: *The entrance to the firm in 1905.*
Right: *Making cups and bowls circa 1931.*

During the first year of business at Tunstall a distinctive Union Jack logo was designed, a logo which is still in use today. The Tunstall name was incorporated into the mark which immediately identifies it as being an early Weatherby product. At Hanley the wording on the Union Jack logo was changed to 'Durability'.

Over a very few years business grew rapidly and in 1906 the company built a new three story building containing offices and a show room where the firm's expanding range of products were on display.

John Henry Weatherby died in 1933 leaving his sons Samuel & John Henry junior to run the firm and guide it through the difficult years to come. During the second world war like many other businesses the firm suffered from the loss of skilled workers into the armed forces. And worse, pottery firms were given production quotas at a level often far less than they needed to continue in business. Inevitably during that period some firms found they could not continue and closed, selling their quotas to other companies. Fortunately Weatherby's survived to be carried on by yet another generation of the family: John Stuart Weatherby and John Lucas Weatherby - and eventually a fourth generation when John Stuart Weatherby's sons Christopher Stuart and Jonathan Richard Weatherby joined the firm. Christopher is now Chairman and Managing Director and Jonathan is Sales Director.

Today Falcon Potterys' main markets are hotel ware, catering ware and giftware which are sold throughout the United Kingdom and overseas. The next time you are abroad on holiday turn over your plate and who knows, you may find an unexpected reminder of Hanley!

Top: *Staff in the packing house around 1931. The warehouse manager Tom Broome is pictured on the left. He lost his arm during the first world war.*
Above left: *Placing saggars in the oven circa 1931.*
Below: *Managing Director Christopher Weatherby, left and Sales Director Jonathan Weatherby, right.*

Flushed with success

One place we can all be guaranteed to visit every day is our bathroom. And when we do there is an excellent chance that we will make use of products manufactured in Stoke-on-Trent. Astonishingly, however, Trent Bathrooms is now the last remaining vitreous china sanitary manufacturer in the area.

The 'Trent Sanitary Works' were founded in 1896 by Johnson Bros, a family firm already manufacturing both tableware and bathroom products. Johnsons built several factories, including the Trent works in Hanley, one of the townships in Staffordshire which in the early years of the 20th century were amalgamated to form the city of Stoke-on-Trent.

In the previous two hundred years scores of potters had set up their workshops in the valley of the river Trent to take advantage of the ready supplies of clay which was a by-product of a then thriving local coal mining industry. The area soon became known throughout Britain and the world as the 'Potteries', the heart of the British ceramics industry.

What an unexpected treat it is for connoisseurs of nostalgia to browse through the Johnson/Trent back catalogue and be reminded of such still faintly familiar and evocative names as the 'New Royal', 'Imperial' and 'Victorian' bathroom suites. And how surprising to discover, or be reminded, that in the late Victorian and Edwardian period a 'lavatory' was not a water closet but in fact a hand basin.

In the first half of the 20th century Johnson Bros and 'Trent Ware' established themselves in the UK and in many export markets as bywords for quality and service. During the 1960s the whole of Johnson Bros business was acquired by Wedgwood, that other famous potteries company. Wedgwood's own subsequent merger with the Irish glass manufacturers Waterford in the mid-1980s led them to concentrate on their core business of tableware and to sell their bathroom interests. This led to the purchase of the Trent Sanitary works by Shires Limited in 1987.

The Shires Group is one of the three major British bathroom product manufacturers with around 1,000 employees at five factory sites: two ceramic production units in Stoke-on-Trent (the Trent Works in Hanley and a second pottery built by Shires in 1975 in Longton); one fireclay factory in Lancashire (Shaws of Darwen); a shower enclosure factory in Rochdale and an acrylic bath production site in Bradford, Yorkshire.

Above: *An early wash basin produced by Trent.*
Below: *An advertisement showing a range of bathroom ware.*

Trent Bathrooms is managed as a trading division within the Shires Group with sales and marketing strategies distinct from those of its sister division Shires Bathrooms. The Group's manufacturing sites supply products specified by the two divisions to meet the requirements of their separate distribution channels in the UK and abroad. In most areas Trent Bathrooms and Shires Bathrooms sell to different market sectors and this 'dual brand' policy enables the group to be more responsive to market trends and opportunities around the world.

The most recent initiatives managed by the Trent-based commercial team have been the development of the 'Shaws of Darwen' fireclay brand relaunched in 1996 with the addition of high-style 'Shaws Original' range of traditional sinks; and the introduction in 1997 of a distinctive new bathroom brand, 'The New England Bathroom Company' offering innovation with traditional English styling.

With access to the Group's substantial manufacturing resources, widely recognised to be at the leading edge of technological progress in the industry, Trent Bathrooms can justify and maintain its strong reputation for product quality and customer support. Its product portfolio, constantly under review and redevelopment, offers sanitaryware, baths and accessories in fourteen colours for commercial and domestic use including many products which have been engineered to meet the plumbing standards of Trent's export markets.

Trent Bathrooms have been manufacturing sanitary ware for well over a century now. The firm's practice of using flint for an improved finish and enhanced durability has from the outset given the business a reputation for quality. The Trent name can be found in many of our grandest old buildings as well as prestigious modern projects such as the Montevitro Centre, the St James Homes Development and the refurbished Windsor Castle. This is one firm at least that can prove it is no flash in the pan!

Above centre: *Two early stamps.*
Top: *The company's premises in the early 1900s.*
Right: *The Waverley Suite.*

Automation came to the potbanks as in any other business. Here, dust pressing wall tiles, the woman is part of the industry that the general public often forgot. There were countless tile making firms in the city in the 1940s and 1950s. Outsiders only think of decorated vases and pretty ornaments with raised reliefs when considering the Potteries. Tiles were made by the million. Walls, floors and ceilings all over the world are covered in the wares that poured out from the factories. Table tops and work surfaces have been tiled with Potteries produced goods for decades. Still, the image of the Etruscan figures and delicate dinner services persists. This woman wears a headscarf that dates her in the middle years of the 20th century. It was a cheap head covering and was useful in keeping out the dust and grime from that Toni perm. In the 1950s, Queen Elizabeth II went out wearing one, though in a different style. That gave the headscarf royal approval. We do not know what wage this woman earned, but she was not on the top rate. The best paid females worked in the painting and decorating bays. There they produced pretty and popular designs. One of the most famous was the Wedgwood Fairyland series in the 1920s. Elves and pixies were all the rage as people sought a magical escape from the depression years.

ware as being 'A fine black porcelain, having nearly the same properties as the basalts, resisting the attacks of acids; being a touch-stone to copper, silver and gold and equal in hardness to agate or porphyry.' Josiah did not believe in using one word where several dozen would do!

Top: On her visit to the Etruria works in 1941 Mrs EJ Warrillow was shown round the Black Basalt Room by Tom Simpson and Mary Thornton. She admired the popular style of pottery that had been made since 1768. It was in August of that year when Josiah Wedgwood completed his experiments in turning out his new stoneware. His Black Basalt was a class above the similar products of his competitors. The smooth surface with its shiny black sheen was an immediate hit with the general public. The factory was hard pressed to meet the demand that flooded in for all manner of candlesticks, vases, medallions, ornaments and tableware. Stoneware was similar to earthen-ware, but was fired to a higher temperature. This made the finished product non porous and stronger. Powdered flint pebbles, brought up the Trent and Mersey Canal that passed the door of the Etruria Works from the east coast, gave substance to the firing process. As Tom explained all this to Mrs Warrillow she was probably expecting to be tested on her new knowledge when she got home. Ernest JD Warrillow MBE was an associate of the Royal Historical Society and Fellow of the Society of Antiquarians. He went on to write a number of children's short stories, but is best remembered for his large work on the social history of Stoke-on-Trent. He would have been pleased to see Mrs Warrillow sharing his passion for the life of the Potteries.

Above: This is not a picture of a cottage or some simple stirring of the embers in any old firegrate. The old stools and fire irons in this room can tell a story going back over 200 years. In 1941 Mary Thornton was posing at the original grate in Wedgwood's Black Basalt Room. There had been a tour of the premises and she was demonstrating how the grate had been used in the days when Black Basalt was the company's most famous product. It was the first ornamental body that old Josiah Wedgwood had developed. He was quoted as saying, 'The Black is sterling and will last for ever.' He was not the first to produce a black body. Several earlier potters had developed one called 'Egyptian Black'. As with everything he did, Josiah was determined to turn out the best he possibly could. He put his heart and soul into developing a fine grained black stoneware that could be seen to match the Etruscan vases that were being uncovered in archaeological digs. He described his

This is typical of any photographer, but especially true of a man. He has not been content to shoot the women sorting the biscuit fired tiles as they would be normally. The prettiest one has been pulled to the front and posed where she can be isolated and show a pretty calf at the same time. She has put on a clean overall for the picture and what about the shoes? That was hardly her everyday working footwear. She must have been tipped off the day before. More typical of the sorting bay is the state of the wall beyond. Peeling whitewash and cracked brickwork made it a gloomy working environment. Sorting the tiles before they went off to be glazed was not the best job to be had. It was usually poorly paid women who had to take on these jobs. The best money was in the more skilled painting and decorating rooms. In terms of numbers, the potbanks employed men and women on an equal basis. The division of labour was far from that. Men and women seldom worked side by side. The firing and loading work was a male province. In Victorian times children were employed here. They were regarded as mini adults. Children started work as young as seven or eight. Many were literally worked to death. They had a 12 hour day and 30 per cent did not survive to see their 15th birthday.

Right: Whilst the ballroom at Trentham Gardens acted as a bank clearing house, the mail had to be sorted before it went any further. Outgoing communications passed through this area, as well. The foyer had never seen such activity. Tons of paper passed across its tiled floor as it was turned into the post office and paymaster general's section. The numbers on the wall were not put there to help the workforce choose the next hymn. They were there so that the women could accurately sort the mail into huge bags, before it was moved on to the next department or the outside world. Post Office Court in London was too vulnerable to attack from the bombing raids that the government knew would come. A direct hit could lead to complete confusion if important documents were destroyed in transit. Trentham Gardens had several advantages. Communication links were good. It was also not in an area likely to be targeted by the Luftwaffe. In 1940, Trentham Gardens was home to a company of French Legionnaires. General de Gaulle visited them in his role as leader of the Free French forces. They had fought in Norway, struggling to keep back the advancing tide of the German army. This Allied campaign was a failure. After early successes, the troops were poorly supplied and lacked the right equipment for the Arctic conditions. After the shambles, the veteran Tory MP Leo Amery stood up in the House of Commons. He snarled at Prime Minister Chamberlain, 'In the name of God, go!' He did. In came Churchill.

Below: Whatever you do, never refer to the woman second left as a member of St John's Ambulance Service. All those who give freely of their time in support of others know that is the wrong title. It is the St John Ambulance Service. The black and white uniforms turn up at every event where large numbers of the public gather. There is always a tent at grand shows or a station set up at an open air event. Trained in first aid techniques, the service members deal with wasp stings, grazed knees and broken limbs. No injury is too small for them. None is so serious that they do not know the correct and potentially life saving initial treatment. During the war, St John joined forces with the British branch of the International Red Cross to provide food and comfort parcels for prisoners of war in foreign camps. A 1942 poster showed a soldier behind barbed wire, clutching a packet of goodies. 'A bit of home' was the poster's slogan. It hoped to encourage those of us who were safe and secure to send something to keep up the spirits of the POWs. The selfless workers were pictured with a representative of the LMS railway on Stoke station. Soon the hampers would be loaded onto the train and be making their way to the brave lads overseas. The Red Cross was the brainchild of Jean-Henri Dunant, a 19th century Swiss. Its work was honoured in 1944 with the award of the Nobel Peace Prize. The award was repeated in 1963.

The ballroom at Trentham Gardens rocked to the sounds of 'Please, please me' and 'Get off my cloud' in the 1960s. The Beatles and Rolling Stones were just two of the top line acts that played this venue. Today it has many uses. They range from grand balls to trade fairs. During the war the walls rocked to the sound of adding machines rather than guitars. It was used as a major clearing bank centre. The financial cogs of the country had to be kept well oiled. Safe from the London blitz, row upon row of desks were attended by female clerks moved up from the capital or specially recruited from local labour. Although war was not declared until 3rd September 1939, on 26 August two special trains left London. Almost 900 bank staff piled on board. In a matter of days, the ballroom was transformed into a hive of monetary activity. Barclays, Westminster and Midland banks were sited here, with Lloyds out on the balcony. It was almost exclusively a female operation. The whole programme ran with military precision. Mounds of paper, bundles of cheques and piles of drafts were processed with the same efficiency these women had provided at home base. The adding machines look antiquated to those of us brought up in the computer age. These were the original number crunchers. Their skilled fingers flew across the numeric keys and pulled little handles to calculate the result of their input, all measured in pounds, shillings and pence.

Above, both pictures: It took a lot of work to rebuild the Theatre Royal after the fire that gutted it. In a single hour the roof caved in and the whole interior was ablaze. These 1950 workmen were trying to put back together a building that has had a varied career. Once a Methodist chapel, it was built on the site of an old mine winding shaft. A centre of entertainment since 1841, it finally returned to use as a theatre in 1982. After these builders had finished, it would see service as a cinema and bingo hall. Critics of the British workman would have enjoyed this scene. Arms resting on scaffolding poles, plenty of standing around watching or lounging on the end of a pickaxe, but only one or two actually doing some back bending. It all gives the impression of a slow job. Flat caps were the only head protection that these men had. The day of the safety helmet had not yet come. People passing by had to watch out for their own safety. Anyway, if they were daft enough to walk under the scaffolding, that was their look out. The shot of the workmen is scary. They must have had a good sense of balance. Up in the roof area of the Theatre Royal, they were demolishing what remained of the fine old theatre that had been ravaged by fire the previous year. Rebuilding work would find the Royal, as it has become called, open up again in 1951. Known as the 'Potteries Own' or 'People's Own', its stage had been trodden by top line acts and players for a century. On the night the theatre burned down, Sadler's Wells world famous ballet troupe was due to appear. Fortunately, the dancers were not on stage when the fire took hold. If so, only 'The Firebird' by Fokine and Stravinsky would have been appropriate! After reopening, the Royal had a chequered career. It opened and closed and served as a cinema and bingo hall and then once again a theatre. The Regent has taken over its role as the centre for more highbrow events. In the theatre's early days, it was home to a Chartist's meeting room. Chartism was the first movement both working-class in character and national in scope. It grew out of the protest against the social injustices of the new industrial order in Britain. One of its leaders, Feargus Edward O'Connor, toured Britain. Angry supporters clashed with the establishment in the Stoke riots of 1842. But, as Victorian prosperity grew, the movement's effect declined. However, most of its social reforms were eventually adopted.

The Co-op opened its dairy on Shelton New Road in 1929. It had its own body shop. Vehicles were customised from transporting meat into being milk floats. The brand spanking new Model A Fords shone brightly in the sunshine. They replaced the horse drawn vehicles that had previously trundled around the streets. A lot of the business was taken up in supplying milk to local schools. Every morning playtime, children in the primary school tucked into a third of a pint of good nourishment. After the second world war every single local authority had to provide free milk to schools. It was a way of improving the health of the nation's youngsters. Every morning they sat cross legged in a circle in front of the teacher. The straw monitor handed round the little cardboard tubes that we used to suck up the goodness. There always was one little monster, usually a boy, who blew bubbles. He was promptly scolded. It was a daily ritual. Straws and bottle tops were never thrown away. Another monitor collected them. They were given to the washing monitor for cleaning. Later that day they reappeared in the art and craft lesson. The naughty lad of morning playtime was now allowed to do blow painting. When Margaret Thatcher became Minister of Education in the early 1970s, free milk was taken away from schools. She was called 'Thatcher the milk snatcher'. The little bottles made a comeback in the 1980s, but many authorities made a charge for the service.

The Warrillow Collection

Left: In 1949 even manual workers kept their hats on. Not for them the stripped to the waist style of digging. They were there to do a job, not display their suntan and muscles. The flat cap was the indicator of social class. It was the sign that you did a proper job and got your hands dirty. Theirs was not the namby pamby world of the office and the pen pusher. The chap centre stage is, perhaps, after the glory of being the focus of the photograph. His headgear places him in the ranks of the bosses or chargehands, at least. Whilst to some it might appear he was putting the jam into a giant doughnut, there is a real significance to what is taking place. This is the laying of the plinth of Trubshaw Cross in Burslem. As the others beaver away behind him, our happy chappie is getting ready for the erection of the memorial that is soon to appear. Situated by Newcastle Street, the small garden around the memorial was being prepared. When springtime came this corner would be awash with colour. It stood as a contrast to the bottle ovens peeking over the roofs of the houses in the background. For years they had gushed forth the smoke and grime that were as unattractive as they were unhealthy. However, they paid the rent. Still, it was nice to have a tidy little oasis of Mother Nature on this. It would have been such a pity to put up a memorial and leave it stark and bare without adornment to soften the scene.

The golden rule for success

Goodwins the Jewellers have been part of Hanley for more than 125 years, and the business today combines the traditional craft skills of jewellery-making with the ability to create designs to suit modern tastes. Readers may remember - or even be fortunate enough to own - a set of the 'Cup-Links' which the company manufactured to commemorate Stoke City FC's victory in the 1972 League Cup Final; this limited edition of personalised gold cufflinks is a perfect illustration of the way in which Goodwins continue to delight their customers.

The family business was established in the Potteries in 1874 by Charles Edwin Henry Goodwin. Charles came from a family of jewellers and learnt the trade in his father's shop in Manchester, back in the days when shops were expected to stay open until 10pm on Saturday night. Father and son both specialised in clock and watchmaking, while the sale of wedding rings formed the most important part of the retail business. In 1874 Charles Edwin moved to the Potteries and started his own business at 12, Hope Street, Hanley. In due course his own son, Charles Percival Morgan Goodwin, joined the firm, and when number 16 Hope Street became available, Charles Percival bought it.

Operating as jeweller and watchmaker from the two premises, the business continued to grow, serving the needs of its customers as best it could even through the difficult war years. The main problem during the war was the serious shortage of 22ct wedding rings, and often long queues would form outside the shop in the hopes of being able to secure one of the few which were available.

Charles Percival took the business over from the founder in 1912, and in 1959 he handed it down to the third generation. Charles David Goodwin was interested in jewellery manufacture, and before long he seized the opportunity to acquire numbers 14 and 16a Hope Street and make the premises into one. This was an event of some significance, resulting as it did in pleasant, spacious premises with room to expand the manufacturing element, and 12-16 Hope Street has remained the home of Goodwins, Jewellers, ever since. Although the shop is situated outside the main retail centre of the town, trade has never suffered because of this, and the great advantage of the Hope Street premises is that jewellery can be manufactured in the workshops adjoining the retail shop - something that would not be possible in a prime High Street location.

***Above:** Mr C E H Goodwin, seated is pictured with his family, Mr C P M Goodwin is standing, 1916.* ***Right:** Mr C E H Goodwin, founder, standing outside his shop at 12, Hope Street, Hanley.*

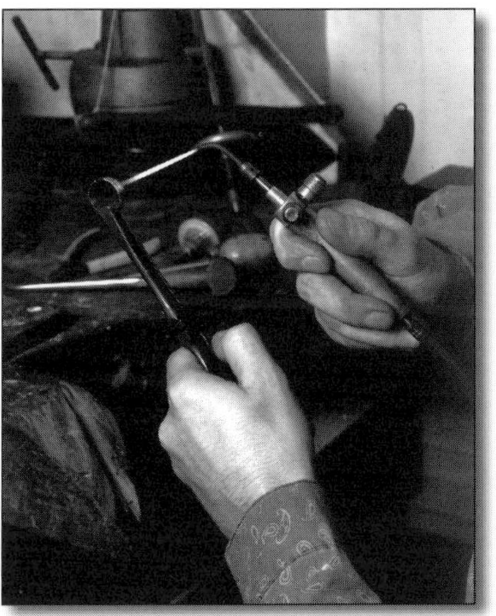

In the early 1980s Charles David Goodwin's two children entered the business - Susan Jane in 1983, and her brother Charles Phillip Mark the following year. The three of them worked together for some 15 years, with Charles Phillip practising as a goldsmith and Susan working in the office and shop. Charles David retired in 1997, and sadly both he and Charles Phillip died the following year, leaving Goodwins in the hands of Susan Goodwin and her mother, Mavis.

Retail, repair and manufacture all remain important aspects of the work at 12-16 Hope Street. Goodwins' manufacturing business is known in trade circles as G & S Jewellery, and is a regular exhibitor at major shows, such as the one staged annually at London's Earls Court. The entire manufacturing process is carried out on the premises, from the initial casting through to the setting of diamonds and precious stones. Jewellery is still made in a very traditional manner in many respects; although equipment has been modernised to some extent, many of the tools have not changed since Great Grandfather Charles Edwin Henry Goodwin's day, and it is still the experience skills of the hand craftsman which ensure the quality of the finished item. Goodwins make their own distinctive range of contemporary jewellery and supply jewellers throughout the country with a range of Victorian reproduction jewellery, and expert repairs are also carried out in the workshop.

The same high levels of expertise are reflected in the retail side, where staff have superior product and technical knowledge as well as excellent interpersonal skills. Service is tailored towards helping a customer make the right choices in a personal and non-pressurised manner. Customers include young couples getting engaged and long established customers going back several generations; all are more than happy to make the short journey to Hope Street to find top quality service and products at the most competitive price. Goodwins' unique range of stock can provide the perfect answer for somebody looking for 'that something special', whether contemporary or classical.

Goodwins is a long-established family business with long-serving, expert and friendly staff, whom customers have come to know and trust. Its aim for the 21th century is simply to maintain and enhance the traditions and reputation established by previous generations, bringing beautiful jewellery to the Potteries.

Above left: *One of the firm's goldsmiths at the bench.* ***Above right:*** *A locket manufactured by Goodwins.* ***Top:*** *An exhibition stand at Earls Court.* ***Right:*** *Sue Goodwin, Charles David Goodwin and Charles Philip Goodwin pictured on the occasion of Charles David's retirement in 1997.*

Diamond - A history to be proud of

"Unique" is how The Diamond Tile Company Limited in Hanley is described by customers from all over the world, and what was once a Victorian pottery firm with four bottle ovens is today one of the most prestigious home interior showrooms in Britain, with over 70 of the finest colour co-ordinating fully tiled room settings of Bathrooms, Kitchens, Bedrooms and Fireplaces.

The Company was registered on the 11th May 1932, by five friends who decided to buy the derelict pottery firm and start the manufacture of tiles for fireplaces. The Company was run by RHC (Harry) Cliff a pottery factor who was destined to be part of the company for the next 35 years.

A year later Harry Cliff's daughter Dorothy left school at the age of 14 and joined the firm to help her father in the office. Later, she married Tom Staton whose family name eventually became indelibly associated with the firm.

Dorothy says that when she started work the wall mounted telephone rarely rang more than twice a day. How times have changed! Most documents then were written by hand and the only form of heating in the office was a black stove pot.

In those early days in Diamond Tiles' office Dorothy recalls that she was not too good at spelling, but she did have a good head for figures and so concentrated on looking after the books. It soon became Dorothy's job to pay out the wages on a Friday morning - Dorothy also had the unpopular job of locking the door at ten past eight each morning: anyone who had not clocked on by that time had to wait until 8.30 before being admitted and would have their pay docked accordingly.

In pre-war days the firm employed around a hundred people and used four bottle ovens for making tiles. Dorothy remembers that in those times before radio and piped music had made their way into the workplace the 'makers' and 'dippers' employed by the firm would sing as they worked, sometimes in loud competition with each other.

Every few months during the 1930s the firm would use its ovens to fire new tiles. The ovens would be fired for a whole week and unemployed men were then taken on as casual labour, stripping to the waist before climbing into the hot interiors to hand down 'saggars' the clay boxes in which the tiles were packed for baking.

Despite the economic depression of the 1930s people were beginning to become more houseproud and the firm was thriving, selling fireplaces all over the country including Ireland.

Dorothy Cliff met her future husband Tom Staton before the war. Tom was from a family of butchers who actually lived near the firm's premises in Century Street, at that time Tom was the manager of Price's National Teapots at Longport.

T C 'Tom' Staton joined the Diamond Tile Company in 1941 just before he and Dorothy were married. Typical of the times, Tom left to join the RAF the day following the wedding and was away for the duration of the war. No doubt Tom's safe return from the war was an event both longed for and long awaited by his young wife.

At the beginning of the war the Ministry of Supply commandeered the company's warehouse to store bales of hessian for camouflage.

Above: *Dorothy Staton and her husband Tom on their wedding day in 1941.*

In 1943 Tom Staton became a shareholder in the business, when the war ended and there was a huge demand for fireplaces for the new houses being built he decided to start manufacturing tile fireplaces as well as the fireplace tiles. Fourteen years later Tom and Dorothy bought out the remaining shareholders and made the firm a true family business.

When in 1967 Harry Cliff retired, Tom and Dorothy decided to switch the focus of the firm from the manufacturing of fireplace tiles to the manufacture of feature fireplaces and in 1961 Tom patented his own design called The Kingsley "Hole in the Wall" fire, which had the fire opening eight inches above the floor and a wider fire opening. This meant people could have a raised hearth and plinth in stone, slate or marble on which they could put a television or ornaments. By 1968 Tom had designed the first centre of the room fireplace to burn coal and logs, this had a large canopy to draw the smoke up through the flue and out of the chimney. The Kingsley "Hole in the Wall" and Centre fires proved very popular and were sold all over the British Isles as well as being exported abroad.

Dorothy stayed and worked for the ministry, keeping records and sorting out the deliveries and collections. The company then took a complete change of direction. With the outbreak of war china dolls could not be imported from Germany and the local hospital, desperate for presents to give the children at Christmas, asked if the company could manufacture dolls for them. Tom had the moulds made while home on leave from the RAF. Harry then arranged production of the parts, while Dorothy and her mother Florrie strung the dolls joints together, painted the dolls faces and dressed them in baby clothes. The 'Diamond Pottery Doll' was a huge success and soon the large toy shops, including Harrods, were buying as many as the firm could produce. Unfortunately four years later the family had to stop manufacture, when they were no longer able to use colour to spray the dolls because of wartime regulations.

All the designs were manufactured and displayed at the premises in Century Street, Hanley and when the showroom needed to be increased in size, Tom decided it would be a good idea to display a few tiled bathrooms and kitchens so that he could sell them to his customers who were building new houses.

Top: *The Diamond Tile Works in 1935 showing the bottle ovens.* ***Above:*** *The Kingsley patent "Hole in the Wall" design, CS 100.*

Later, part of the old buildings were demolished so that a large customer car park and new entrance from Marsh Street was made and a new retail look was given to the remaining buildings.

The business expanded and the sales of Bathrooms and Kitchens gradually took over from Fireplace manufacture as the Company developed to what it is today, a Premier showroom with expert staff who design and install the very best quality products available from the worlds leading manufacturers.

Sadly, Tom Staton passed away in 1985, Dorothy however remains as Chairperson of the company although Susan Adams, who joined the firm in 1973, has now taken over from her as Company Secretary. Dorothy, despite being over 80 years of age, still goes to the office for several hours each day, a habit difficult to break after more than 60 years of working for the firm.

Carol Staton, Tom and Dorothy's daughter and a successful business woman in her own right, has been at Diamond for almost 30 years since leaving school. As well as looking after her son and daughter, running the company and developing the export side of the business, Carol designs the showroom displays and manages the bathroom and fireplace divisions of the company, "Designer Bathrooms" and "Traditional Fireplaces". Director and designer Chris Bentley is in charge of the kitchen and bedroom division, "Kitchens of Distinction" and "Bedrooms by Design" and Director Simon Jolley specialises in the company's tiling division by supervising the tile trade department and retail showrooms, as well as organising the company's tiling contracts.

Diamond is a very special family business, the Directors, designers and sales advisors design clients homes to express their own personal requirements, creating rooms which are comfortable and a pleasure to live in. All the staff work together to give the best, friendliest service possible. Carol says "my father created the best showroom in the area, and due to the hard work and dedication of all Diamond's excellent staff the company is now one of the largest and most superior home interior showrooms in the UK, with clients from all over the world and an unrivalled reputation for quality and service. I know he would be proud of what we have achieved".

Top: *The Kingsley "Monaco" Centre fire.*
Above: *Dorothy Staton proudly displays one of the dolls made by the firm at the beginning of the war.*

Going strong in soft furnishing

What a time to start a business! 1941...the darkest days of World War II when Britain stood alone against Hitler. But that was exactly the time Elizabeth Cartlidge chose to launch her bold venture.

You would have thought 36 year old Elizabeth had enough to do as a busy housewife and mother, contributing to 'the war effort'. But drawing on her experience in the family fruit business and with indomitable drive, she set off on her business career.What a long way it now seeems from this humble beginning to the prosperous and expanding Cartlidge's soft furnishing businesses in Hanley and Crewe!

Elizabeth used her family's thriving fruit shop in Brook Street, Cobidge, as her first base. After only two years, however, she was able to transfer to the bustling Hanley Market. And now you will find Cartlidge's in the market below the modern Potteries Shopping Centre as well as the Hanley shop.

It wasn't long before Elizabeth's children began helping her in running the businesss. Eventually, her four daughters and one son all became fully involved. Expansion was inevitable and a further shop was opened in Lichfield Street and then another in Crewe in 1981. Now a third generation helps to continue the proud family tradition.

Not everything has been plain sailing, though. Elizabeth recalls one Christmas when the Lichfield Street branch was flooded and all the stock spoiled...and that at the busiest time of the year! And there were the five years of 'temporary relocation' between the demolition of Hanley Market and the opening of the new Potteries Shopping Centre.

Throughout its 60 year history the company has prided itself on its care and experience in soft furnishings. If you can't find the item you want on the shelves a made-to-measure service is readily available for your home, office, pub or hotel.

The Cartlidge soft furnishing story is still continuing to unfold. A fleet of vans now helps to supply customers' needs throughout Staffordshire and Cheshire. The firm's original horse and cart transport of the war years would struggle to cope with its modern workload!

Above: *Company founder Mrs Elizabeth Cartlidge celebrating her 90th birthday.* ***Below:*** *The premises at 15 Piccadilly Arcade.*

A stunning aerial view of Hanley which was taken in the late 1950s

Acknowledgments

The Warrillow Collection, Keele Information Services: Library, Keele University

The Potteries Museum

Alan Taylor

Syd Bailey

Thanks are also due to
Andrew Mitchell who penned the editorial text
and Steve Ainsworth for his copywriting skills